What Your Colleagues Are Saying . . .

"Daniel Bauer has the ability to deeply engage others in how to be better leaders, share what he has learned in the process, and offer it in a book. *Mastermind* is not just engaging from the first sentence; it offers research and practice that can help us have a deeper impact on leading and learning."

Peter DeWitt, Leadership Coach
Author, *Collective Leader Efficacy* and
Instructional Leadership
Albany, NY

"Daniel Bauer has created incredible communities for educational leaders worldwide. In this fun-to-read, inspiring, and practical book, Danny shares with us his rationale for starting mastermind communities and how he designs this specific type of professional learning for leaders. You learn how masterminds can create tremendous growth for all who participate."

Jennifer Abrams, Communications Consultant
Author, *Stretching Your Learning Edges: Growing (Up) at Work and Having Hard Conversations*
Palo Alto, CA

"When we are isolated we are not fully aware of the possibilities. Daniel does an amazing job in *Mastermind* revealing what new perspectives offer. Leaning in on unbiased trusted advisors opens the door for unlimited opportunities. Don't miss this one, school leaders."

Aaron Walker, Founder
View From the Top
Hendersonville, TN

"Though Bauer's book is about how masterminds allow K–12 leaders to reach their potential, I recommend it for those in higher education as well. As a college president, I rely on the tools Bauer highlights: opportunities for mentorship, investment in personal growth, a push for innovation, support networks, and the capacity to see challenges and issues through multiple perspectives."

Hilary L. Link, President
Allegheny College
Meadville, PA

"Bauer reveals how isolation, lack of trust, and inadequate professional growth opportunities not only limit the influence of a leader, but even worse, could propel them to leave the profession altogether. The mastermind concept coupled with his ABCs of powerful professional development™ provide the roadmap all school leaders should follow to ensure they develop the support and connectedness they will need to thrive and not just survive."

Joseph Jones, Superintendent
New Castle County Vocational Technical
School District
Executive Officer of TheSchoolHouse302
Newark, DE

"As a university professor devoted to teaching excellence, I'd heard of masterminds but didn't know what they did or value. Daniel Bauer explains them, who does them, why, how, and what to expect from them, illustrated with stories from principals and educators who did them. Now I want to do one. I wish I'd read this book a long time ago."

Joshua Spodek, Professor
New York University
New York City, NY

"The concept of a mastermind has long been a way leaders not only transferred knowledge but deepened their own understanding. Especially during a time of global uncertainty, this is an essential book for school leaders to learn how to use their collective experience to grow. Daniel Bauer takes concepts like 'trust' and 'mindset' and provides actionable ways to build these skills in yourself and others."

Anthony Kim, Author
The NEW School Rules: 6 Vital Practices for Thriving and Responsive Schools
Las Vegas, NV

"School leadership is tough, isolating work. In *Mastermind*, Daniel Bauer spotlights the urgent need for school leaders to connect with a supportive cohort of peers so they can grow, get help with the challenges they face, and anchor their work in deeply held values. No one has done more to help leaders connect with each other and continually challenge themselves to be their very best than Danny."

Justin Baeder, Director
The Principal Center

"In his book *Mastermind: Unlocking Talent Within Every School Leader*, Daniel Bauer masterfully teaches the true power of creating a mastermind group to become world-class school leaders. From conducting difficult conversations to creating a vision, and so much more, Daniel has created a powerful playbook to unlock your highest leadership potential."

Tommy Breedlove
Wall Street Journal and *USA Today* Bestselling Author, *Legendary*
Roswell, GA

"Unfortunately, school leaders are the educators who receive the least professional learning in the building. No more! This book—one that reads like a casual conversation, laughing with a trusted colleague—opens up a transformative approach to growing the leaders of our schools. Join Daniel Bauer to learn about a bold new approach to growing leadership skills."

Jenn David-Lang, Editor
THE MAIN IDEA
Brooklyn, NY

"Leading with a mastermind mindset is now more than nice, it is a necessity. In *Mastermind: Unlocking Talent Within Every School Leader,* Daniel Bauer shares practical tips from extensive knowledge and research on the impact of becoming a better leader and building better schools. Educators will walk away with tool sets, skill sets, and mindsets that will enhance their practices tomorrow."

Jessica Cabeen, Principal
Author, *Lead With Grace*
Austin, MN

"A consistent theme from educational leaders is how isolating the work can be—how alone they feel. A powerful antidote to that is to join a community of peers that illuminates perspectives on education-related issues. If you're looking for a surefire roadmap on how to engage in such conversations, look no further. *Mastermind*—an artful blend of research-based principles and real-world practices."

Jeff Ikler, Director
Quetico Leadership Coaching
Forest Hills, NY

"Every school leader should read this book, and every school leader deserves to be in a mastermind group. Not only does Daniel Bauer outline the qualities of a great school leader, but he also defines the specific ways that we can grow together as a community of learners. At its core, this book reimagines the professional growth experience that school leaders need to be effective in their roles. A must-read!"

T. J. Vari, Assistant Superintendent
Appoquinimink School District
Executive Officer at TheSchoolHouse302
Newark, DE

"If you are not currently participating in a mastermind group, Daniel Bauer gives compelling reasons why you should be. He shares the necessity and importance of connecting with others in order to reach our maximum potential. The reflection questions, assessment tools, and visuals make this book an interactive learning experience. As you read, enjoy a growth opportunity at your fingertips!"

Sanée Bell, Author
Be Excellent on Purpose: Intentional Strategies for Impactful Leadership
Cypress, TX

"This is a must-read for educational leaders looking to transform antiquated public learning systems. Transformation starts within and around other like-minded leaders. Bauer's approach to professional learning is a game-changer."

D'Andre J. Weaver, Superintendent
DeSoto ISD
DeSoto, TX

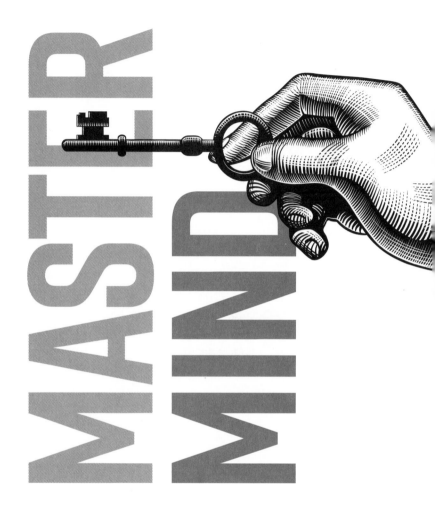

MASTER MIND

This book is dedicated to all the Ruckus Makers who allow me to live out my dream. It is a pleasure and privilege to serve you. Let's keep making positive change in education.

MASTER MIND

Unlocking
Talent Within
Every School
Leader

DANIEL BAUER

FOREWORD BY PAUL BAMBRICK-SANTOYO

A JOINT PUBLICATION

AASA
THE SCHOOL SUPERINTENDENTS ASSOCIATION | CORWIN

FOR INFORMATION:

Corwin
A SAGE Company
2455 Teller Road
Thousand Oaks, California 91320
(800) 233–9936
www.corwin.com

SAGE Publications Ltd.
1 Oliver's Yard
55 City Road
London, EC1Y 1SP
United Kingdom

SAGE Publications India Pvt. Ltd.
B 1/I 1 Mohan Cooperative Industrial Area
Mathura Road, New Delhi 110 044
India

SAGE Publications Asia-Pacific Pte. Ltd.
18 Cross Street #10–10/11/12
China Square Central
Singapore 048423

President: Mike Soules

Associate Vice President and Editorial Director: Monica Eckman

Senior Acquisitions Editor: Ariel Curry

Senior Development Editor: Desirée A. Bartlett

Senior Editorial Assistant: Caroline Timmings

Production Editor: Tori Mirsadjadi

Copy Editor: Liann Lech

Typesetter: Hurix Digital

Cover Designer: Janet Kiesel

Marketing Manager: Morgan Fox

Printed in Canada

Library of Congress Cataloging-in-Publication Data

Names: Bauer, Daniel, author.

Title: Mastermind : unlocking talent within every school leader / Daniel Bauer; foreword by Paul Bambrick-Santoyo.

Description: Thousand Oaks, California : Corwin, 2022. | Includes bibliographical references and index.

Identifiers: LCCN 2021031861 (print) | LCCN 2021031862 (ebook) | ISBN 9781071837085 (paperback) | ISBN 9781071837078 (epub) | ISBN 9781071837061 (epub) | ISBN 9781071837054 (ebook)

Subjects: LCSH: Educational leadership—United States. | School principals—United States. | School management and organization—United States.

Classification: LCC LB2805 .B336 2022 (print) | LCC LB2805 (ebook) | DDC 371.2/012—dc23

LC record available at https://lccn.loc.gov/2021031861

LC ebook record available at https://lccn.loc.gov/2021031862

This book is printed on acid-free paper.

21 22 23 24 25 10 9 8 7 6 5 4 3 2 1

Contents

Foreword

by Paul Bambrick-Santoyo

The juggler has much in common with the modern-day school leader. Both are skilled at keeping multiple balls afloat, and both can make the work seem so effortless that all we see is an arc of balls seemingly suspended in perpetual flight.

But turn your attention to what happens after the routine ends. The juggler somersaults, neatly collects the balls, and exits. The show is over, and all is well. The school leader, in contrast, is still at it. The juggling seems to be perpetual, with an abundance of differently sized and weighted balls, making it nearly impossible to keep them all in flight. As they fall—one by one or all in a heap—some leaders see those dropped balls and resolve to do a better job juggling tomorrow. Perhaps they will hand off a ball or two to the assistant principal or juggle a few more observations. Although they will continue to juggle daily, they're often finding themselves overcome with frustration—and sometimes, despair—in the face of the repeated pattern of drops. And the stakes are so much higher than for a juggler: when the leader falls short, students and staff do as well.

Daniel Bauer steps into that space of frustration and sense of failure and offers a way out. He doesn't do so by offering a guide on how to do this alone (school leadership is a lonely enough job as it is!). Rather, he proposes that we do this together. Daniel's mastermind is powered by the belief in teamwork: a cohort of like-minded school leaders who come together to improve their leadership. Through a foundation built on authenticity, belonging, and challenge, mastermind members push each other to become the leaders their school communities need. At the Leverage Leadership Institute, I have witnessed firsthand the power of school leaders practicing and problem solving as a community. When leaders get better together, everybody wins.

At its heart, the mastermind is an authentic community that challenges and inspires. Thank you, Daniel, for bringing the mastermind concept to the education field and creating a space for leaders to learn from and be supported by one another. Each time we do this work together, we remind ourselves that we are not alone and we find the power in community.

Acknowledgments

The reason the Better Leaders Better Schools mastermind exists is because I experienced it firsthand at View From the Top. Because of that, I am indebted to my mentor, Aaron Walker, for creating *Iron Sharpens Iron*. My own cohort is named "The Legacy Builders," and I'd like to acknowledge the current members who push my leadership to the next level: Charlie Cichetti, John Cole, Stu Brandon, Pat Lordo, Mark Nichols, Trace Blackmore, and James Mills. Thank you to former members of our community as well, especially Jonathan Bates, Anthony Woolever, Scotty Neal, Joshua Elliott, and Keith Harris—rest in peace, my brother.

Three coaches who have helped me dream bigger during this project: Jared Angaza, Tommy Breedlove, and Wayne Herring.

To the other edupreneurs who push me and generously share wisdom: Jennifer Abrams, Jethro Jones, Justin Baeder, and Anthony Kim.

Everyone at the altMBA who helped me clarify "What's it for?" and "Who's it for?": Alex Peck and Marie Schacht; my head coaches, Pete Shepherd (Noodles), Aray Till (Colorful), Rick Kitigawa (KA-BLAM!), Lisa Lambert (Woof), and Rebecca Channer (Owl); my first coaches as a student, Conor McCarthy and Cat Preston; my co-coaches, Michelle Welsch, Eve Stankiewicz, Eric Moeller, and Stacy Richards; and the rest of the altMBA coaches, including Ainsley McCaskill, who specifically encouraged me on this project.

The fantastic Corwin team led by Ariel Curry made this all possible. Thank you for inviting me to make a ruckus by sharing this work. Thank you also for challenging me to create a second draft that was more tightly organized. This challenge is what inspired my breakthrough idea, "The ABCs of powerful professional development™."

The Better Leaders Better Schools team takes care of day-to-day operations so I can create: Abby Santiago, Željko Tomić, Dragan Ponjević, Christina Lufrano, Derek Archer, Katie Novak, Michael Smith, and Laura Correa.

Current Better Leaders Better Schools mastermind members are the reason this book exists. You give me the opportunity to live out my dream each day.

Celebrating our current mastermind members . . .

No Pockets: Colin Hogan, Kathy Jo Standefer, Kyle Borel, Shbrone Brookings, Clayton Reedie, Jason Dropik, Ellen Herman, Franklin Day, David Beard, Nick Hoover, John Mathews, Cassie Gannett, Eryn Smith, Jicela Soto, and Jessica Gamble.

Purple Cows: Philippe Caron-Audet, Melody Stacy, Luke Beilke, Paige Kinnaird, Sofia Hughes, Brandon Ray, Celia Wise Cooksey, Anita Brady, Rhianna Giffin, Eugene Park, Jesse Rodriguez, Bill Marble, Kirk Rickansrud, Linda Fussell, and Christiana Smith.

Free Spirits: Jessica Cabeen, Karine Veldhoen, Suzanne Mitchell, Loren Brody, Nancy Alvarez, Beth Wartzenluft, John Middleton, Chris Horton, Erinn Fauteux, Fran McGreevy, Dana Goodier, Kim Gibbs, Sheila Diaz, Patrice Henry, and Bill Renner.

Guiding Principals: Fred Holmes, Brandon House, Chris Jones, Chris Loeffler, Demetrius Ball, Amy Platt, Chris Jackson, James Jordan, Scott Long, Erica Fleeman, Alex Fangman, Chris Carlson, Lizzy Neiger, Ben Jones, and Tim O'Leary.

Redefining what it means to be courageous, daring, and strong: Andi West, Melissa Gleason, Kristen Craft, Jess Hutchinson, Rebecca Tiernan, Mary Jo Walker, Regina Collins, Kendra Chapman, Tracey Runeare, and Melissa Peterman.

Edupreneurs: Mitch Weathers, TJ Vari, Michelle Goldshlag, Joe Clausi, Rob Breyer, Lindsay Lyons, and Francois Naude.

One-on-one leaders: Kyle Wagner, Sarah Van Brimmer, and Mo Ali.

A special place in my heart is reserved for former mastermind members who contributed to this adventure.

Always and endless thanks are due to my family: the Pertells, Murtaughs, and Bauers. Thank you for your love and support. And to my Zimbabwean side of the family, ndinotenda zvikuru, ndinokudai mese.

Alba, you are a cute puppy. Thank you for making me stop writing from time to time to go out for walks and allow good ideas to come into my head.

And most of all, to my amazing wife, Shupi. Your support is everything dali wangu. Ndinokuda. Now that this book is out, let's celebrate. Which country do you want to visit next?

About the Author

Daniel Bauer is the Chief Ruckus Maker at Better Leaders Better Schools (BLBS). He launched his *BLBS* podcast in September 2015. With over one million downloads, the *BLBS* show is the most influential podcast available for educational leaders. In 2016, he changed how professional development is offered to school leaders through the structure of a mastermind. Since then, Daniel has coached and mentored over 100 school administrators from every continent in the world.[1] In 2017, Daniel launched *The School Leadership Series*, his second podcast, which amplifies the diverse voices in school leadership today. He is the author of *The Better Leaders Better Schools Roadmap: Small Ideas That Lead to Big Impact*, which released as an Amazon #1 new release. Daniel's Just Cause is "to connect, grow, and mentor every school leader who wants to level up." Reading this book helps move his Just Cause forward, and sending it to your colleagues in educational leadership helps even more.

---

[1] Except Antarctica, of course.

"Here's to the crazy ones, the misfits, the rebels, the troublemakers, the round pegs in the square holes . . . the ones who see things differently— they're not fond of rules. . . . You can quote them, disagree with them, glorify or vilify them, but the only thing you can't do is ignore them because they change things . . . they push the human race forward, and while some may see them as the crazy ones, we see genius, because the ones who are crazy enough to think that they can change the world, are the ones who do."

–Steve Jobs

Introduction

*"Experience is not what happens to a man; it is what
a man does with what happens to him."*

–Aldous Huxley

Alarming Trends

A massive study of all principals in Texas from 1995–2008
found three alarming trends in educational leadership.
First, although principal retention varies, elementary
schools have the highest retention rates, while high
schools have the lowest rates. Second, high school leader
retention rates are abysmal. Just over 50 percent of newly
hired principals stay for three years, and less than 30
percent stay for five years. Finally, and most alarming,
about 90 percent of those leaving a school actually leave
the principalship altogether. Principals from this study
weren't leaving one school to go to another; rather, a
majority of principals left the profession entirely (Fuller &
Young, 2009, p. 17). Principals are leaving the profession
for what they have identified as a better situation, and
when they leave, they're gone for good.

The good news is this: districts can use coaching programs to reduce negative job factors and improve principal retention (Bauer et al., 2019, p. 386). The even
better news: principals and other building leaders can
take control of their own development through the
structure of a mastermind. It is the aim of this book to
show you how to do just that.

What Successful People Do

Successful investor Charlie Munger said, "I believe in the discipline of mastering the best of what other people have figured out" (as cited in Parrish & Beaubien, 2018, p. 14). What Munger knows from experience has also been proven by many researchers. Studies show that collaboration is essential to leadership reform (Sherman, 2005, p. 709). Research also established that formal mentoring programs encourage collaboration and promote a culture of lifelong learning for participants. Not only that, but leadership development programs also lead to greater productivity and a more capable staff (Sherman, 2005, p. 710).

I call this the Big Domino. By investing in the development of local school leaders, not only do you get a better leader, you get a better school. School leaders across the globe are discovering the impact that joining a structured coaching program like a mastermind can have on their leadership and their lives. Throughout this book, we'll meet many of these school leaders and see the impact.

These leaders have occupied the same position that you currently have. That challenge you currently face—someone has seen it before. Although you may *feel* like you are the only leader who is facing "X" problem, the truth is, you're not. There is tremendous value in being able to unpack and solve challenges that all school administrators face at some point with a trusted board of advisors:

- Building ownership of vision

- Designing core values that guide your school's work

- Deciding what the first ninety days of your principalship should look like

- Navigating tough conversations successfully

- Dismantling systemic racism in the system of school

Masterminds are quite common in the business setting—I should know, I joined one in early 2016 before starting one myself. Prior to 2016, I had never heard about a mastermind, but after joining, I realized there was a rich history of masterminds operating in the business sector. Business entities know something schools would be wise to adopt: we'll go further, faster, together. Too many schools pay lip service to collaboration, when in reality they reward competition. It's easy to think "winning" businesses operate this way too, but the truth is, they don't. My mentor credits his business success to the fact that he has been a part of masterminds for decades. He often tells me that he'd rather be "an inch wide and a mile deep versus a mile wide and an inch deep." His mastermind peers have helped him eradicate blind spots and navigate challenges skillfully. Successful people will always figure out a necessary solution, but the most successful realize they have a choice—the much easier independent path versus the more robust collaborative path. A mastermind provides the latter.

One reason successful people continue to be a success is that they build a system that supports their high performance. Blind spots and a lack of perspective get in the way. Our egos and overconfidence harm us. The further we are from a choice we make, the greater the likelihood we will make the same mistake and believe

The further we are from a choice we make, the greater the likelihood we will make the same mistake and believe a false narrative of what actually occurred.

a false narrative of what actually occurred. It is difficult to admit when we lack understanding or are actually incompetent. To ask for help requires safety and courage. Successful people know this, which is why they surround themselves with people who will push them to be better and protect them against their natural weaknesses.

The philosopher Alain de Botton said, "The chief enemy of good decisions is a lack of sufficient perspectives on a problem" (as cited in Parrish & Beaubien, 2018, p. 33). The mastermind presents the perspectives you need to be your best and produce the results that you'll be proud of. You just need to bring yourself and be willing to show up authentically, admit where you need help, and plug into a community of support.

The Origins of the Mastermind

The mastermind concept is not new. In 1937, Napoleon Hill devoted an entire chapter to the concept of what he called a "Master Mind." He found that a mastermind was the driving force behind power and riches.

He defined the concept this way: "The 'Master Mind' may be defined as: 'coordination of knowledge and effort, in a spirit of harmony, between two or more people, for the attainment of a definite purpose'" (Hill, 1937/2005, p. 195). What Hill's definition shows us is that a mastermind is a community where two brains are better than one, or, as he says it, "a group of brains coordinated (or connected) in a spirit of harmony will provide more thought-energy than a single brain, just as a group of electric batteries will provide more energy than a single battery" (Hill, 1937/2005, p. 197).

It was Andrew Carnegie who taught Hill about the mastermind concept. Carnegie used a mastermind to help him create incredible wealth and influence. Some other leaders who leaned on a mastermind in order to be successful include Henry Ford and Franklin Roosevelt (Hill, 1937/2005, pp. 196–198).[1]

The main reason I joined a mastermind years ago was that I heard a Jim Rohn quote on an episode of the podcast *Entrepreneur on Fire*. The host, John Lee Dumas, quoted Rohn, who said, "You are the average of the five people you spend the most time with."

Ouch!

That quote hurt when I first heard it. I couldn't get it out of my mind, and I found it to be true. Back in 2015, when I started to dream what my podcast could become, I wrote a plan in my notebook and showed my closest friends and family.

Their response was generally uniform, either "That's nice" or the more candid, "That will never work."

The Rohn quote challenged me to change who I was spending all my time with. If I wanted to level up and increase my influence, I had to surround myself with other can-do thinkers on a similar path. Note: this doesn't mean everyone will love your ideas or agree with you, nor should they. My mastermind experience has taught me that it attracts the right

---

[1] Ford called his mastermind "The Vagabonds," and Roosevelt called his mastermind "The Brain Trust." I didn't know this prior to starting my masterminds in 2016. Interestingly, I challenged my mastermind cohorts to name themselves as well, so we have names like the "No Pockets," the "Purple Cows," the "Free Spirits," the "Guiding Principals," and "Anavah." I'll share the stories behind these names later in the book.

You might not be as familiar with Roosevelt's mastermind members, but know that they all contributed to him being able to create and execute his "New Deal" for the United States. I bet you've heard of Ford's mastermind compatriots: Thomas Edison, Harvey Firestone, and John Burroughs.

kind of individuals—those interested in "leveling up." Although opinions will differ and personalities will surely clash, by building a community on the ABCs of powerful professional development™, we know that feedback we receive is coming from a trust-worthy place.

Hill (1937/2005) knew this to be true as well: "People take on the nature and the habits and the *power of thought* of those with whom they associate in a spirit of sympathy and harmony" (p. 198).

If Hill is correct, then we need to look no further than the company we keep if we are experiencing lousy results or desire to do something more impactful.

Change your community and you'll change your mind-set. Change your mindset and you'll change your actions. Change your actions and you'll change your results.

Pick your inner circle wisely.

My Mastermind Origin Story

I started my podcast, *Better Leaders Better Schools* (*BLBS*), in 2015 shortly after attending a conference called The Global Leadership Summit. There I heard a quote that changed the trajectory of my life:

"Everyone wins when a leader gets better."

That quote had a weight to it. I felt its responsibility. It reminded me of John F. Kennedy's "A rising tide lifts all boats."

Essentially, my community's ability to prosper was linked to my leadership development. I felt a pit in my stomach. Sure, I was currently at the conference being inspired, taking notes, and making a plan to improve my leadership capacity. But when I looked at the rest of the calendar, it was vacant of growth opportunities.

My lived experience as an assistant principal was this: we did not receive any leadership training at all. It was a blind spot for the district. At that time, the district also didn't develop most of its principals. A few "elite" principals were handpicked for a leadership program facilitated by highly paid corporate consultants, but the majority of the principals within the district were overlooked. When they called us together, the meetings focused on logistics: "Do these ten things to move the school forward or you'll be fired." That last part wasn't said out loud and it didn't need to be. The message was clear.

Later, as a principal, this too was my experience. Principals were called together for nothing more than logistics and bureaucratic platitudes.

Reality was different from the leadership priorities identified by the district. Here are some examples of what I actually needed to know how to do:

- Conduct difficult conversations

- Inspire an organization to move in the direction of the vision

- Handle a student's suicide

- Unpack race and navigate racist curriculum

- Focus on self-care in order to be the best version of myself for my community

Unfortunately, these were not the priorities identified by district administrators or topics on offer for professional development (often shortened as PD).

There had to be a better way to offer professional development to all school leaders. So what started as a personal desire to grow my skill set became a movement that I believe will revolutionize how school leaders are grown around the world.

Welcome to the mastermind.

What You'll Find in This Book

This text is organized into two parts.

In Part I, we will first look at the problem with current professional development models. In order to do this, I'll share both personal observations and anecdotes, as well as what the research says about professional development. My research has found that professional development doesn't work when it is inauthentic, is isolating, and misses opportunities.[2] You will also learn some quick facts about the masterminds I facilitate—who we are, why the mastermind works, and the mindsets of our members.

In Part II, we will do a deep dive into the mastermind model I've created. I call it the "ABCs of powerful professional development™." In my experience, powerful professional development always has these three elements: authenticity (A), belonging (B), and challenge (C). When professional development incorporates each aspect of this model and implements at a high level,[3]

---

[2] This book is loaded with interesting research, real stories from the field, great anecdotes, footnotes (like this one), and maybe even a few surprises along the way. For example, the first person to read the book and post an online review will get a free pizza, just like I did when I read a book, completed a book report, and turned in my reading log at the local Pizza Hut in the 1980s and 1990s! Make sure you send me your review, so I know you were first. Email me a screenshot of your posted review at daniel@betterleadersbetterschools.com. We'll sort the pizza details from there.

[3] Educators love to call this implementing "with fidelity."

it always leads to transformation. And that, Dear Reader,[4] is what makes professional development powerful. Each chapter in Part II will include research, stories, and examples of how to incorporate the ABCs into your professional development.

Shall we begin?[5]

Ichi-go Ichi-e

There is an art to leadership as well as an art to bringing people together.[6] The Japanese idea of *ichi-go ichi-e* is that you only have this moment in time, right now, and then it's gone. Forever.

Ichi-go ichi-e is a gentle reminder to be fully present in this moment. This idea informs how we gather in a mastermind, and it should challenge how you read this book right now. I invite you to eliminate all distractions in your environment and to engage with the content with purpose. I invite you to annotate and make this book your own by writing in the margins and highlighting the text that speaks to you. Whether you read for the next ten minutes or two hours, the next time

---

[4] Would you prefer I call you something else?

[5] Spoiler alert: There is actually one more section before we begin "Part I." But if you think about it, you're already a few pages into the book, so I guess we've officially *begun*. Congratulations for making it this far!

[6] The best book I've read on bringing people together is Priya Parker's *The Art of Gathering*. We read this in 2019 in the mastermind I facilitate. It has been one of the most popular books we've read and I highly encourage the reader to check this book out next. School leaders are gathering people all the time: open houses and other school functions for the community, performances, and internal events from all-staff meetings to smaller departmental meetings. This book will transform how you think about gatherings and will upgrade anything you facilitate. Don't take for granted that people will pay attention and want to attend, just because you put the invitation out there. Parker's text will show you exactly what to do to create remarkable experiences.

you pick up this book, the words will have stayed the same but you will have changed. So seize the moment!

This time we spend together right now is a sacred time. You are investing in your professional growth, and when you close this text and go out to serve your community, take action on an idea here and be a better leader.

And with that, let's look at what makes school leadership challenging and what leaders say they want in professional development.

Mastermind Case Study
Melody Stacy
Principal at Taylor Mill Elementary

"The mastermind is a community of generous leaders who are both courageous and compassionate. Being connected to and learning with these remarkable people continues to push me to fight off the forces of mediocrity in all areas of my life."

Tell us what you do and what your work typically entails.

I am the proud principal, a.k.a. the Believer-in-Chief, at a preschool–5th grade elementary school in northern Kentucky, serving who I unabashedly call "the best team of leaders around." Through an inspiring vision, or shared "why," I work to illuminate a collective path to greatness that unleashes the genius and awesomeness of everyone in our school community. As one of my morning affirmations reminds me, I am here to seek out and inspire the greatness in others, and my unshakeable belief in public education as the best path to bringing hope for a better future leaves me with a clear and strong sense of purpose.

How has the mastermind helped you?

The mastermind has both broadened my perspectives and solidified my belief in what true leadership looks like. There is a special combination within this group that understands and empathizes with the challenges we school leaders face on the daily while holding true to the aspirational journey we need to remain steadfast.

What's the best part of the mastermind?

I have treasured the books we have read and discussed together as well as the relationships we've built. Leaders are voracious learners, and having the opportunity each week to learn within this community is such a huge value-add to me and my leadership. Add to that people I am able to call dear friends and you have a pretty special combination.

What is one way the mastermind has helped you approach leadership differently?

To be able to lay out a new idea or an issue with which I'm struggling and trust that I'll be met with a group that will help me improve and show up as the best version of myself is a steady lifeline in this thing called leadership. Because the mastermind is a community that shares the same drive to create that magical mixture of love and high expectations, it is place that gives me new ideas and a place where I am comfortable being uncomfortable.

What advice would you give a leader considering joining the mastermind?

If you are comfortable with where you are and feel okay with being mediocre, the mastermind is not for you. On the other hand, if you want to join a community that will challenge your thinking while also being there for you, then you just found the world's best PD available for school leaders.

Introduction Reflection Questions

What have you heard about masterminds? What questions do you have about this way of offering professional development?

What does it take to be fully present in the moment right now (*ichi-go ichi-e*)?

Think back to your best PD experience. What made it memorable?

Think back to the PD in which you have participated over the past two years. Did it meet your needs? If so, how? If not, why not?

This book opens with a quote about experience. What does the quote mean to you? What commitments will you make to your professional growth this year?

Part I

1 The Problem With PD

What I've Noticed

"If you do not change direction, you may end up where you are heading."

–Lao Tzu

Figure 1.1   Common Leadership Challenges

Since 2016, it's been my privilege to serve more than one hundred school leaders from around the world in a professional development experience called the mastermind. Over the years, I have found that leaders enroll in the mastermind for similar reasons (listed in Figure 1.1):

- I feel like I'm on an island.

- I don't trust my colleagues (local school and/or district level).

- The job is hard!

- My district doesn't build my capacity.

- My district won't send me to conferences.

- I need support accomplishing my goals.

- I lack a network of peers to admit what I don't know and ask for help.

All of these reasons are significant and important to address. But of all the challenges cited, the most common reason leaders join the mastermind is their desire to grow. Mastermind members want to surround themselves with peers who understand the role, are committed to sharpening their skill set, and want to innovate in education. According to Paige Kinnard, a Director of Instruction at Allegany-Limestone Central Schools, "I want to run with other hungry leaders. People who are passionate about education and willing to do anything in their power to grow."

Three Lines That Explain It All

"Most geniuses—especially those who lead others— prosper not by deconstructing intricate complexities but by exploiting unrecognized simplicities."

–Andy Benoit

For professional development to be profound, it doesn't have to be a high-tech solution or a complex model. The model on which the mastermind is built is simple and powerful. There is nothing complex about it. In fact, it is what I consider common sense, but common sense isn't often common practice. Generally, the answers to questions that haunt us are right in front of us. Leaders who listen to their gut instinct and intuition have an advantage over those who do not trust themselves. I naturally used this model to create a powerful PD experience that serves school leaders. It wasn't until years after launching the mastermind that I codified the model that I call "the ABCs of powerful professional development™."[7]

Figure 1.2 contains another simple idea. It's just three lines that explain everything about what's right and what's wrong with professional development opportunities. Each line represents a continuum. The left represents suboptimal professional development that is inauthentic, is isolating, and represents missed opportunities. The right represents the categories that make up my model and lead to powerful professional development: authenticity, belonging, and challenge.

---

[7] In fact, it wasn't until I started writing this book that I did the hard work of creating this model. After some generous feedback from my editor, I was challenged to organize the content more tightly in this book. Her feedback was right, but it didn't make my job any easier. I wondered how in the world I would address the feedback and organize the book you are reading right now. And then . . . Eureka! I needed a model. So I stopped writing. I took longer walks in nature and let my mind wander. Then I opened my journal and sketched out what I saw on a weekly basis in the masterminds I facilitate. That's how I created the model that ultimately became the book in your hands. I share this story to give you a little history into the process it took to bring this book to you, but I also share it as a leadership tip. Whenever you are stuck, it doesn't make sense to keep working on the challenge in front of you. It's better to (literally) walk away from the challenge and get away from the project. Listen to your inner wisdom and I promise that you'll find what you are looking for.

Figure 1.2   The Professional Development
                      Continuum

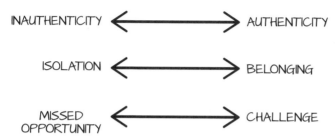

The closer you get to the ABCs, the closer you are to creating a transformational experience. The further you are from the ABCs, the further you are from real impact. I also humbly suggest that you need to be strong in all three areas for truly transformational experience. Two out of three aspects are good, but not good enough. In professional development design, keep pushing until you are strong in all three areas. This is why the community I facilitate, the mastermind, works.

In the rest of Chapter 1, we will explore the three challenges that limit the effectiveness of professional development offered to school leaders: inauthenticity, isolation, and missed opportunities.

Inauthenticity

"If you bring forth what is in you, what is in you will save you. If you do not bring forth what is in you, what is in you will destroy you."

–The Gospel of Saint Thomas

What Stops Us From Evolving?

Professional development designed for school leaders often misses the mark because of inauthenticity. Some common and poor leadership advice is to separate the personal and the professional. In many schools, the leader operates as a robot keeping their staff distant. This is a mistake. People crave authenticity. They want to know what drives you as a leader and where the organization is going.

The inauthenticity problem also extends to the professional development offered. The most egregious example of inauthentic professional development is when it's absent altogether or offered sporadically. Instead of a "ready, aim, fire" approach, many districts get the order wrong and instead follow the inconsistent model of "ready, fire, aim." You don't have to be a rocket scientist to know this misses the mark of professional development.[8]

Whether it is a fitness goal or learning a new skill, like playing the piano, piecemeal professional development is the quickest way to exhaust resources while generating little momentum. This kind of professional development is not leverageable. It does not lead to internalization, action, and results. Simply put, this form of professional development does not work.

This form of professional development is inauthentic because it fails to *see* the administrators it aims to serve. Another reason that professional development offered by districts (or invested in by districts) is inauthentic is that it is siloed. School leaders decide to enroll in it because they are seeking diversity of thought.[9] Some leaders may ask, "Am I the only one who thinks this way in my district?" These leaders experience friction

---

[8] I checked with some friends at NASA and they agree this claim *is not* rocket science.
[9] A typical mastermind cohort at Better Leaders Better Schools includes leaders from all levels of education and experience, and from not only various states within the United States, but also various countries. Not only that, we are diverse in terms of gender, sexual orientation, religion, ethnicity, and any other way you think about demographics.

in terms of applying new and innovative ideas that will help education evolve. Without the support of other innovative peers, these leaders often are frustrated to the point of giving up or leaving the profession entirely (Fuller & Young, 2009, p. 17).

Internal professional development opportunities do not address this issue; they only exacerbate the problem by creating an echo chamber that favors a confirmation bias—"We're the best district! Our ideas are amazing!"—which slows down progress and educational evolution. Therefore, this kind of professional development is inauthentic.

I'm sure you've heard the definition of insanity, which is often misattributed to Albert Einstein: "Insanity is doing the same thing over and over expecting a different result." No matter who said it, the idea applies here to the lack of evolution regarding professional development. Much change is needed in education, but when you consider the leverage produced by developing leaders, few would argue that any other change would have a better return on investment.

Think about it. Discipline has evolved and many schools are using a restorative approach. Assessment has evolved and schools have shifted to mastery or standards-based grading. The failed zero-tolerance discipline model has been replaced by more effective programs focused on prevention, threat assessments, and restorative practices (American Psychological Association Zero Tolerance Task Force, 2008, pp. 853–856).[10] Instruction has evolved and students

---

[10] Zero tolerance is one of the worst ideas ever used in education. It doesn't lead to better results or even a safer community. The offending student doesn't learn the lesson from the mistake made. Rather, the student learns that the school or district doesn't want them around anymore. The only appropriate use of zero tolerance is applied to zero tolerance itself. This idea in education needs to die!

are engaged with project-based and authentic problem-based learning. Teacher collaboration evolved with the introduction of professional learning communities (PLCs). But how has professional development, specifically designed for school administrators, evolved? It hasn't for most districts, and as a result they offer professional development that is experienced as inauthentic by its leaders.

Canadian neurologist and astronaut Roberta Bondar said, "So how does a business survive in constantly changing environments? When change hits, a common response is denial or trying to adapt with a business model that no longer works. We can influence the outcome of changing environments more rapidly by first recognizing that we actually need to survive and then moving to survive with new ideas" (as cited in Parrish & Beaubien, 2019, p. 216).

The same could be said for education. A lack of innovation creates inauthentic professional development. Another reason professional development is stagnant is a lack of professional awareness.

Listen to the Older Fish

In 2005, author David Foster Wallace gave the commencement speech to the graduates of Kenyon College. Below is an excerpt from his speech and book:

> "There are these two young fish swimming along and they happen to meet an older fish swimming the other way, who nods at them and says, 'Morning boys. How's the water?' And these two young fish swim on a bit, and then eventually one of them looks over at the other and goes, 'What the hell is water?'" (Wallace as cited in Parrish, 2012).

Professional development offered within a district can fall into the trap that the fish in Wallace's story experience. They don't even realize they are swimming in water! What a grand lack of awareness! There is a reason corporate executives, world-class athletes, and musicians hire coaches. An outside opinion matters when a leader wants to level up and operate at peak performance. Without an outside perspective, the data received are faulty; they are inauthentic.

Blind spots and echo chambers can be deadly for a leader's development, impact, and ultimate success. Being ingrained in a culture for years where everyone looks, talks, and thinks the same has an adverse effect on the type of leadership needed to be effective in an increasingly changing educational landscape. Like the fish, school administrators have difficulty separating the forest from the trees. They do not even realize that they are swimming in water. Possibly, they have forgotten what the point of education truly is—to expand the minds of students, afford them access to knowledge and experiences that wouldn't normally come their way, and generate productive members of society who will make the world a better place.

Far too many districts get swept up by the politics and pleasing of the school board and parents over serving the students. Some districts are hypnotized by test scores and make illogical decisions like extending the school day and cutting arts and physical education to make space for more reading and mathematics instruction. They believe this will lead to better student performance, but in reality it is a faulty assumption.[11]

Without an outside perspective, the data received are faulty; they are inauthentic.

---

[11] Simply practicing more doesn't lead to better outcomes, especially if the quality of instruction is poor. Practicing the right way under the tutelage of an expert leads to better outcomes. Additionally, we all need time off "to blow off steam." As an adult, I love to learn, and a good portion of each day is spent studying and writing. I also protect

The mastermind acts as the older fish. Outside perspective is a generous gift. The majority of members end up joining our group because they know they will hear perspectives that don't exist in their districts, and those perspectives are invaluable and authentic.

A lack of perspective hurts, but what happens if the older fish never appears? What if the two young fish continue to swim each day and never realize that they are in water? When that happens, you experience what experts call an "echo chamber."

I Can't Hear You in an Echo Chamber

Professional development is also inauthentic when designed in echo chambers. Sherman (2005) found that internal leadership development programs can support the status quo (p. 710). Similarly, Carmeli and Gittell's (2009) research notes that learning within organizations is often a single loop. This is unhelpful in that errors are identified and corrected, but the root causes are ignored and go unchallenged (p. 711). Humans are notoriously bad at admitting mistakes. Kahneman and Tversky's (1979) work on risk aversion and prospect theory found that humans experience mistakes and loss two times worse than what it feels like to be right (pp. 264–269).[12] This leads to an "Everything is great" attitude that

---

space for creative pursuits like drawing and playing the guitar, as well as making sure I do something active each day. By taking time off to let my mind wander or engage my creative side, my body and mind are able to reboot. When I do return to work, I return fresh and ready to engage at a high level again. Our kids need this, too.
[12] Daniel Kahneman (2011) is the author of *Thinking, Fast and Slow*. We read this in the mastermind, and although it is dense, it is a great guide to understanding how the human mind works and the cognitive biases that hamper our thinking. Eileen, if you are reading this, I'm glad you enjoyed Kahneman's work so much!

nurtures a blind-spot-riddled, echo-chamber culture, and fosters inauthentic professional development.

We've all experienced this and it is incredibly frustrating. Every district—from the best to the worst—can suffer from creating an echo chamber. In some respects, this may be a result of strong leadership. If a leader communicates the vision well, if the people understand it and then start to act on the vision, it may become the only reality that exists. It is very difficult to share concerns or to show why a plan might fail in some districts. When groupthink exists and everyone talks the same way, there is little room for diversity of thought. You've heard the Abraham Maslow quote: "If all you have is a hammer, everything looks like a nail." Welcome to the echo chamber.

An echo chamber hampers the collective wisdom of a group or organization. Inauthentic professional development also exists when it doesn't challenge leaders to expand their circle of competence.

Expanding Your Circle of Competence

In 2015, I joined a mastermind called Iron Sharpens Iron. The personal and professional growth I experienced in a short amount of time was tremendous. My knowledge, expertise, and, ultimately, success accelerated. This experience led to an epiphany—*who is doing this for educational leaders?* And so, the mastermind was born.

Why did I experience such tremendous growth in a short period of time?

My circle of competence grew. By leveraging the combined experience of my mastermind colleagues, I was able to learn in months what life had taught my peers over decades.

There is an anonymous quote that illustrates this point perfectly: "Learn from the mistakes of others. You can't live long enough to make them all yourself."

Smart and persistent leaders eventually sort out their problems and figure out the challenges they face. But why take the longest route when a more efficient route exists?

According to Parrish and Beaubien (2018), there are three key practices to build and maintain a circle of competence: curiosity and a hunger for learning, monitoring, and feedback.

All leaders who enroll in the mastermind exhibit the first practice. They are extremely curious and lifelong learners. The mastermind helps in the second and third aspects of growing your circle of competence.

The mastermind helps with monitoring because it provides the structure and systems to identify goals and track progress. Parrish and Beaubien (2018) offer an interesting perspective: "[We] have a problem with honest self-reporting. We don't keep the right records, because we don't *really* want to know what we're good or bad at. Ego is a powerful enemy when it comes to better understanding reality"[13] (p. 64). This confirms what Kahneman and Tversky found in their research mentioned earlier.

The space we create in the mastermind is one where everyone is equal. We don't compete for position, authority, title, or attention. We also don't judge one another, and it helps that we don't work in the same school or district. Because of that, leaders can be

---

[13] If you'd like to learn how to be a more honest self-reporter, I adapted a decision journal from Parrish's work (2014) and it's included in the Resources section (and my website for download/reproduction). I've used this decision journal on some major decisions. It's a leadership game changer and just one example of how we serve leaders within the mastermind.

radically honest about their performance, which allows the mastermind to deliver on the final point of a circle of competence—feedback.

When I peer out into the world, I do not see my face. Without a mirror, I have no idea what I look like; in fact, I might not even know I have a head if it wasn't for the mirror![14] The world just appears in the space where I am told my head exists, and it's with this perspective that I seem to be at the center of everything.

This is an unhelpful and self-obsessed way to operate in life and leadership. By seeking out external feedback, I learn two important truths: I do, in fact, have a head, and I am not at the center of the universe!

The mastermind is built to offer external feedback, help its members see what they cannot see, and offer multiple loops of feedback with helpful data that give leaders the chance to develop.

We've all gone out to dinner before, only to get home and notice that we have spinach in our teeth. Upset, we wonder if who we met for dinner are even our friends[15] if they let us go through the night with food wedged between our teeth. In the mastermind, we tell you when you have spinach in your teeth so you can show up as your best.

Inauthentic professional development is one of three problems that hamper the experience often offered to school leaders. In the next challenge we will look at an equally dangerous hurdle most leaders face—isolation.

---

[14] According to Douglas Harding, I actually don't even have a head. For a wild adventure into mysticism and philosophy, check out Harding's *On Having No Head*. It might just blow your mind.

[15] They're not your friends. They're just acquaintances. Or maybe they're educators who notoriously hate conflict. And spinach!

Isolation

"It's hard to read the label from inside the jar."

—Joel Weldon

"I feel like I'm on an island. Even in New York City surrounded by other people. It's easy to exist in a bubble and I'm looking for new ideas and what other school leaders are doing around the world to be their best."

—Patrice Henry, Purple Cow member 2021

Two Years Is a Long Time . . .

How would you rate the professional development you receive in your district? Is it building your capacity and supporting your needs? Do you have access to a powerful network of outstanding colleagues who understand the complexities and challenges of your role? Or do you feel like Patrice and countless other leaders—surrounded by other people, but isolated in terms of who you can reach out to for support?

Levin et al. (2020) surveyed school leaders and found some troubling statistics. Of the 407 elementary principals who responded to their survey,

- 32 percent spent time sharing leadership practices with peers three or more times in the past two years,

- 23 percent had access to a mentor or coach in the past two years (and only 10 percent of principals who served in high-poverty schools had access to a mentor or coach), and

- 56 percent participated in a PLC three or more times in the past two years (p. vii).

Districts are failing to provide the support principals need in order to grow. This is alarming given the significant impact principals have on their schools. Although this study focused on elementary principals, we can generalize those findings to the secondary level as well.

The statistics are troubling and illustrate the lack of access to professional development and a network of peers. Isolation is a major factor in leadership stagnation, which is crazy! Of all the human beings in the school, the leader is crucial to school and ultimately student success. Why do leaders lack access to quality professional development and a network of peers?

Levin et al. (2020) also found that 84 percent of principals they studied faced obstacles to pursuing professional development. The top three obstacles were

- a lack of time (67 percent),

- insufficient building coverage (43 percent), and

- not enough money (42 percent; p. vii).

The majority of school leaders who enroll in the mastermind at Better Leaders Better Schools note that they operate on an island and are looking for connection, coaching, and mentorship. In order to grow their leadership skills, school administrators need access to a high-quality network of mentors and peers who regularly meet throughout the year. Three or more times is not sufficient. If your doctor participated in professional development less than three times in the past two years, would you still trust them with your health? If school leaders are not meeting regularly, what is the impact of isolation on their development?

If your doctor participated in professional development less than three times in the past two years, would you still trust them with your health? If school leaders are not meeting regularly, what is the impact of isolation on their development?

Isolation Is the Enemy of Excellence

It boggles my mind that leaders still operate in isolation. In Greg Salciccioli's book *The Enemies of Excellence*, the reader learns that the first and biggest enemy of excellence is isolation. We learn as children that "two heads are better than one." Intuitively, we know that it's better to have support in leadership. So why do so many leaders go it alone?

There are a multitude of factors at play. Some leaders are merely afraid to ask for help. Fear and shame prevent them from requesting help because they are afraid of being found to lack competence in an area or want to avoid appearing that they don't have the answer. Some leaders are like a hamster on a wheel, leading a frenzied life. These leaders don't make time for lunch, let alone asking others for help! Other leaders battle the problem of overconfidence and ego. After all, as the boss you were hired to be a problem solver.

Leaders who operate in isolation are destined to make more mistakes than those who lead within a powerful network of peers. Worse yet, these mistakes are preventable.

In the section on inauthentic professional development, we looked at how leaders develop blind spots and struggle to be honest with self-reporting.[16] Every leader I know has blind spots. That's normal. If you could see your blind spots, well, they wouldn't be blind spots. Leaders are generally hard workers and great at a few things. This is their circle of competence. Every specialist has a circle of competence and that's a good thing. After all, most people don't go to a physician for investing advice.

---

[16] If you eat healthy and work out consistently, why don't your pants fit anymore? Really?

As school administration has grown more complex, it is impossible for leaders to be competent in every area. Yet many leaders are asked by districts to lead the way in instruction, management, finance, and marketing, just to mention a few of the hats principals wear. The mastermind is an invitation to grow your circle of competence and eliminate blind spots by substituting connection for isolation.

Unlike some districts, everyone in the mastermind is cheering for your success. We also don't evaluate our members. Therefore, we are free to share tough feedback and criticism in order to make each other better. We don't work together, so there are no messy politics to navigate. There is an application process to join, so we only enroll leaders in the mastermind who are hungry, humble, and smart.[17] Cassie, an assistant principal in Colorado, recently joined because she needed a push to get better that she wasn't receiving in her district.

Not only are many school leaders starving for honest critiques on how to improve their leadership, but individuals are also terrible at being honest with their own weaknesses. Within the mastermind there is nowhere to hide. As long as a member commits to showing up authentically, they can count on other members to push them to grow. As a result, their circle of competence grows. They are no longer leading in isolation, and with a trusted board of advisors who want them to succeed, they know they can turn to the mastermind at any time in order to make the best decision for the school community they serve.

It is difficult to maintain a circle of competence without an outside perspective. Even more difficult is finding an outside perspective that you can value and trust as a

---

[17] According to Pat Lencioni, these are the qualities of top performers. I suggest you check out his book *The Ideal Team Player* for more.

school administrator. Even if you do have this network, meeting just a handful of times over two or three years will not lead to growth. The mastermind succeeds at Better Leaders Better Schools because we connect leaders from around the world who are united in their desire to get better and to participate in a community where everyone is committed to their own development and the success of others. We meet consistently and challenge our biases, decisions, and assumptions in order to grow.

We See You. We Hear You.

Principals are leaving the profession for a number of reasons. My experience has taught me—and research has shown—that principals leave because of the stress involved in the position, poor district leadership, unrealistic demands and expectations, and an inability to make the change they are committed to (versus what the district wants them to do).

I think all of those reasons principals leave could be eliminated if districts invested more time and energy into seeing and hearing their principals.

When districts treat principals as a replaceable part, or a cog in the system, it is easy to leave that kind of culture. This happens through poorly planned and executed policy that is tone-deaf, representing low emotional intelligence. It also pushes principals further into isolation. If leaders don't feel safe, the natural thing to do is withdraw, or what Brené Brown calls "armoring up."

The Pareto Principle teaches us that 20 percent of our actions drive 80 percent of the results. Upgrading the relationships between district and principal as well as investing in leadership development are areas where districts could level up their cultures and performance. I believe relationships and leadership development are the 20 percent that lead to results.

If districts would stop obsessing over test scores and attendance data, and instead focus on relationships and leadership development, then I promise the student performance improvement would follow.

In the mastermind, we don't come with an agenda of what to accomplish. The members are our agenda. We meet them where they are and serve them there. Funny thing about that approach—the results follow.

We build in processes to keep track of what happens within our meetings. We don't allow members to hide. We call out our peers when they've made mistakes, and we do this all from a place of love. Leadership thrives in a space where people can be themselves and are fully accepted for what they bring to the table (more on this in Part II of the book).

Consider Renee's experience. She's a veteran educator who recently completed her first year of the principal-ship. Renee is attuned with her need to be connected as a leader, and during her second year as a principal, COVID-19 hit.

Renee wrote during the summer planning amidst the pandemic, "I need strength. Reassurance. Maybe just to call it what it is and move on. Who knows? I feel I'm caught in the middle of my emotions and I can go either way. I'm not used to having a problem with no idea of what I need to get through it. Right now I feel like I'm standing on a frozen body of water and it's only a matter of minutes before the ice starts cracking. Therefore, I'm afraid to move. I'm a mover and a shaker so immobility kills my spirit."

What I wrote to her was a simple text. It said, "The ice won't crack beneath your feet."

She responded, "Awww. Thank you, Danny. I always appreciate your encouragement."

Little emotional quotient (EQ) touches like this mean so much to people you serve. It communicates "I see you. I hear you. You are important to me." Not only did Renee experience that simple text as a way of being acknowledged, but she also knew that she had a powerful community that she could lean into, so even if the "ice began to crack," we wouldn't let her drown in the icy waters of isolation.

In the introduction, I noted the alarming percentage of principals who leave the profession. Bauer et al. (2019) have found that the complexity of the role and the challenges of the principalship are seen as out-weighing the benefits of the role. Principals also feel solely responsible for the results of the school, which often leads to isolation. This isolation can be eradicated through the vehicle of social support like a mastermind (pp. 384–385, 394).

The Problem With Blind Spots

How does an isolated leader fix what they cannot see? Leaders need trusted advisors who can point out the natural blind spots we all have. It is truly an excep-tional experience when a leader builds a team that will tell her what those blind spots are. Even more radical is a leader who demonstrates courage by acting on the feedback they receive in order to grow.

Charles Darwin said, "Ignorance more often begets confidence than knowledge" (as cited in Parrish & Beaubien, 2018, p. 72). A confident leader must open themselves up to a feedback loop in order to sharpen their skill set and eliminate their blind spots.

One mistake I made as a new principal was a direct result of having a blind spot. Building culture is a strength and passion of mine. I prioritized celebrating achievements when staff members did something exceptional at school. I also wanted to honor our entire staff for living out our core values. To do this we formed a culture team, set up a process where staff could nominate their peers to win a culture award, and then we would celebrate them at our regular staff meetings.

This process had worked well at previous schools I led, and I expected the same at this new school.

After a few weeks of celebration, a veteran teacher spoke privately with me and let me know that the majority of the staff didn't want to be celebrated and felt uncomfortable with the celebrations. She had established clout within our school; she had taught for decades, was the math department chair, and served on several key committees. Believing her, I rolled back the celebrations at our school, only to find out this upset *the majority of the teachers!*

What was going on here? Was this teacher untrustworthy?

No, I had a blind spot and didn't investigate what she had told me.

I had been fooled. This veteran teacher had not spoken for the entirety of the staff, but rather a small subsection of teachers, if that. Maybe she only spoke for herself, and after I eliminated our celebratory culture, many teachers were upset that they weren't being celebrated. I could have easily avoided this mistake if I had brought the scenario to a network of peers. I am certain if I shared the context of what I was trying to accomplish and what the veteran teacher told me, that I would have been given helpful and critical feedback from my mastermind peers. They would have asked questions such as the following:

- Had I checked in with a variety of staff to test the validity of what the veteran teacher told me?

- Was there value in continuing to celebrate even if teachers were uncomfortable? Was this a way to help them grow (think: Vygotsky's Zone of Proximal Development)?

- What was the benefit of celebrating a smaller set of teachers? How could I continue to honor them?

- Why did I bring this process to the school? Why was I wanting to abandon it so quickly? Did it have enough time to catch on? How was I communicating the vision?

The mastermind would have asked me these questions and more. My thinking would have slowed down and I can guarantee that I wouldn't have rolled back the celebrations at my school so quickly. This may seem like a minor decision and blunder, but it represents how poorly we can make decisions as leaders when we go it alone.

Inauthentic experiences and isolation are two reasons professional development fails school leaders. The last reason professional development can fall short has to do with missed opportunities. There are plenty of ways we can grow and support school leaders. The opportunity is there for the taking, so why do districts so often miss the boat?

Missed Opportunities

Start close in,

don't take the second step

or the third,

start with the first

thing

close in,

the step

you don't want to take

—David Whyte, "Start Close In"

Printed with permission from Many Rivers Press, www.davidwhyte.com. David Whyte, "Start Close In," *David Whyte Essentials,* © Many Rivers Press, Langley, WA USA.

The Power of Reframing

In 2020, my wife and I joined our best friends in Scotland, Simon and Korkor, on a hike of "The Whangie." Simon is an intelligent and lanky Scotsman who loves to laugh and dance.[18] He can hike a mountain in just a handful of strides. I nearly had to sprint each mountain we hiked together. Korkor is a free spirit, warm and strong. They make a perfect match and have two of the sweetest boys in the world.

If you know anything about the United Kingdom, and specifically Scotland, you know that it is nearly/most likely/usually/universally wet. This day was a wet day too, but it was also cooler than normal and that meant one thing for our hike—ice.

---

[18] And like any respectable Scot, enjoys whisky too. To Simon I owe my love of drinking Lagavulin while singing "Loch Lomond" or "Fairytale of New York."

About ten minutes into the hike we hit the ice. And for the next two hours my wife and I took turns walking a few steps before slipping and falling down—often! In fact, my wife swore then to never go on a hike with me again.[19]

Just like mistakes, no one likes falling down. Earlier in this book, I mentioned how humans experience loss two times greater than we experience success. It doesn't help when districts pretend to value learning from failure when, in reality, they treat those who fail with the proverbial "whack!" of a 2 × 4 across their head.

One of the biggest reasons principals leave the profession is that they feel underprepared and overwhelmed by the sheer magnitude of the principalship, which negatively impacts principal retention (Reid, 2020, p. 3).

But there is a solution.

Researchers widely agree that novice principals benefit from mentor relationships and leadership programs (Sherman, 2005, p. 78). I've mentored both novice and veteran principals for years and because of the relationship we've built, they've continued to work with me for multiple years. Mentorship is an easy way to retain school leaders. Connection is key. Relationships are gold.

Ice, mistakes, and failures are all missed opportunities when it comes to professional development and school districts. Zander and Zander (2002) point out that "mistakes can be like ice. If we resist them, we may keep on slipping in a posture of defeat. If we include mistakes in our definition of performance, we are likely to glide through them and appreciate the beauty of the longer run" (p. 101).

---

[19] My wife resumed hiking with me again six months later. By then her aversion to hiking had thawed.

This powerful reframe is an opportunity for all who design professional development. If we truly appreciated mistakes as the mentors they are, then districts could use the 2 × 4s previously earmarked for discipline and reprioritize them for something more useful, like framing a house. A lack of robust mentorship programs that help principals learn from their mistakes is a colossal missed opportunity when it comes to professional development.

Oxygen Masks and Mirror Moments

There is a reason that flight attendants tell their passengers to put their own oxygen mask on before helping anyone around them, including their children, in the case of an emergency. That's because if you don't take care of yourself first—if you don't make sure that you have sufficient oxygen—you're of no use to anyone else, especially when you're dead.

This is hard to do, and hardest for leaders, especially those in education who enter the profession with a servant's heart. This can be a challenge and a missed opportunity because when districts fail to develop their own leaders, it is uncommon for leaders to do this for themselves (Levin et al., 2020, p. vii).

The result is that school administrators would rather invest in the development of their staff than develop themselves. This is the default perspective of most school leaders. If there is a dollar left in the PD budget, that dollar goes to staff members. Can you imagine if businesses operated the same way? I am not arguing that leaders shouldn't take care of their people and provide opportunities for their professional growth. Don't get confused! But that doesn't mean leaders need to be martyrs or starve themselves of development.

As I mentioned in the introduction, the quote "Everyone wins when a leader gets better" changed everything for me. A leader has a moral imperative to make sure that they are getting better. There is a cost to ignoring their own development. In this case, a leader isn't simply standing still. No, while they pass over professional development opportunities, their engaged peers continue to grow. In reality, they are regressing while their peers move forward.

Michael Jordan really started to dominate the NBA when he began to challenge his teammates to improve their game and when he trusted them in key situations. Yet, he did not ignore developing his own skills. I distinctly remember "The shrug" in Game 1 of the 1992 NBA finals, where a formerly mediocre three-point shooter made six three-point shots in the first half alone. Imagine if Michael focused only on his teammates and didn't improve other aspects of his game! That is a ridiculous notion to consider, yet that is the mindset of many school leaders.

One hurdle that leaders must overcome is to choose themselves. To say, "My development is not only important, but necessary to the continued growth of my organization, its staff, and its students." Once a leader makes this mindset shift, they begin to look for opportunities to take their skills to the next level.

Once a leader decides that their development is important and an *unselfish* act, then they must answer an incredibly tough question. I call this the "mirror moment," and to describe it, I'll bring you to a sunny spring day in London.

Eileen was a member of the mastermind for three years before embarking on her dream to sail around the world with her husband. She served as a school leader in China and often went to teacher recruitment fairs around the world to find the best talent. In the spring of 2019, I met Eileen in London to have lunch and to spend time with her after the recruitment fair. At the time I lived in Glasgow, so it was a short flight. More importantly, meeting mastermind members face-to-face is part of my vision because I value relationship building.

We met for lunch at a Lebanese restaurant, one of her favorite cuisines. After lunch we headed out to Kensington Gardens. Eileen was a native New Yorker and tall, so walking with her throughout the park was like a low-intensity jog. We talked about many issues regarding both life and leadership. When the conversation turned to the mastermind, Eileen shared something I had never heard before. She said, "I had to get past the guilt in order to join the mastermind."

Hearing the word "guilt," I wondered if there was something I had done to make her feel that way. If there was, I needed to correct it. Fortunately, that was not it. The "guilt" that Eileen felt had to do with the cost of mastermind membership. It's not a free experience; it is an investment. What Eileen shared is that she invested plenty of her resources to look the part—she bought nice clothes without a second thought. After all, it's important to "look the part" of an administrator.

The mastermind created a type of tension she had not experienced before. Eileen invested in the mastermind out-of-pocket, and before the mastermind she had never made that kind of investment in her own leadership growth. "It was the best professional decision I ever made," Eileen said to me. "After all, looking the part is one thing, but actually being the part is quite another. Looking back, it seems a little ridiculous. Of course how we present ourselves matters. More important than that is our mindset, our ability to make decisions, communication, relationship building, and how we handle conflict."

This story taught me the vast missed opportunity that exists in many districts. With hindsight, it seems crazy that leaders hear a message that makes them believe that it's more important to invest in clothes versus professional development that will improve their performance. Looking the part of a leader is one thing; *being a leader* is a different path altogether.

> Looking the part of a leader is one thing; *being a leader* is a different path altogether.

The Role and the Challenge

Another missed opportunity is helping leaders see what the "right stuff" is to get done. One disturbing trend I see in education is the "hustle culture" and wearing "busyness as a badge of honor."

If you are a leader, you can count on being busy. It doesn't make you special, and it certainly doesn't make you productive or help you add the most value to your organization. There's a big difference between getting stuff done and getting the *right* stuff done. Top performers have the ability to focus and put their energy and resources in doing the right stuff.[20]

I fear that as an industry we are building ineffective leaders who will either remain in the profession and continue to be ineffective or burn out and leave the profession entirely. Both scenarios are unacceptable.

My mentor, Aaron Walker, has challenged me countless times to be an inch wide and a mile deep.

---

[20] Two resources I'll suggest on focus and doing the right stuff would be Gary Keller's *The One Thing: The Surprisingly Simple Truth Behind Extraordinary Results* and Cal Newport's *Deep Work: Rules for Focused Success in a Distracted World.*

Unfortunately, education takes a different approach, producing leaders who are, instead, a mile wide and an inch deep. School leaders are overloaded with responsibility, which interferes with their ability to be a specialist.

Leading a school is incredibly hard work. At times it may even feel like not only are the odds against you, but maybe even fortune and the universe are working behind your back and against you too. It's easy to understand why. In the era of globalization, education reform and the diverse needs of teachers, parents, and other stakeholders are all factors that contribute to the increasingly complex role of the principal (Ng & Szeto, 2016).

There is actually an acronym for this experience that principals know all too well: VUCA, or volatile, uncertain, complex, and ambiguous—also known as *the role of a school leader!*

But not only are school administrators operating in a VUCA world; they are also overloaded with responsibility. Marzano et al. (2005) identify 21 responsibilities considered essential for principal effectiveness (as quoted in Ng & Szeto, 2016, p. 542).

An increasing list of responsibilities and leading within a VUCA environment are increasing the alienation, isolation, stress, and frustration experienced by principals, which then lead to disengagement and flight from the principalship (Ng & Szeto, 2016).

Not only that, but the role of principal is also moving away from traditional planning, organizing, and leading to one of caring and support (van der Vyver et al., 2014, p. 61).

School leaders have a difficult job indeed. But it becomes easier when leaders learn to focus on the *right* stuff and ignore the rest. If everything is a priority, nothing is. One path to higher performance is actually doing more of less. Other industries know this. It may even be considered common sense, but it certainly isn't common practice, which is why this is a massive missed opportunity in professional development offered to school leaders.

Missed Targets and Outgrowing Your Home

When principals in your district get assigned a mentor or coach, what kind of principal comes to mind first?

It's the principal who is struggling—maybe he or she is even on a performance plan. High performers are usually left alone. "If it ain't broke, don't fix it," is the common thought. But that kind of thinking creates a ceiling for performance. Here, good principals never become great, and great principals never become excellent.

T.J. Vari, an assistant superintendent, told me he enrolled one of his district's most talented principals to the mastermind because he had outgrown what the district offered. T.J. has seen the results from this investment as well. The principal he enrolled in the mastermind, Nick,[21] comes back to the district fired up from what he's learning in the mastermind and brings that energy and thinking to the district. He shares what we are doing and what he's learning with his peers. Because T.J. invested in a top performer, all principals are challenged and growing within the district.

In the past when I interviewed for leadership jobs, I loved to ask how a district supported its principals. What I found is that most districts spoke in

---

[21] Nick's case study is available at the end of Chapter 5.

generalities that indicated there wasn't a real plan for nurturing talent within the organization. My experience was that few districts actually provide a robust system of support for high-achieving principals. This thought was confirmed when interviewing Kirsten Reichert and Jeff Ikler on the *Better Leaders Better Schools* podcast.[22] They told me that it's common for districts to talk about leadership development, but when you dig into the actions, you see a misalignment of vision and implementation. John Doerr (2018) says, "Ideas are easy. Execution is everything" (p. 6). Watch what people do rather than what they say. Talk is cheap. Action tells you everything you need to know.

It's also important to note the value of bringing in an outside organization to mentor principals. This helps avoid such pitfalls as central office leaders acting as gatekeepers; discrimination based on sex and race; and internal groups acting as an echo chamber, preserving the status quo, and slowing down growth and innovation (Sherman, 2005, p. 710).

If district leaders ignore the development of their top talent because they think, "If it ain't broke don't fix it," this is a disservice to their top talent. They are causing friction in these leaders' development by accident. This happens in the classroom as well, where poorly performing students are given more attention and intervention, while the top-performing students are left on their own, usually bored out of their minds. What a missed opportunity!

---

[22] Kirsten and Jeff appeared on Season 2 Episode 6. The podcast is titled "Shifting: How School Leaders Can Create a Culture of Change," which is also the name of a great book they wrote also published by Corwin.

Leaders cannot grow when receiving inauthentic professional development, when they operate in isolation, or when they experience missed opportunities. Since 2016, we've been testing our ideas at Better Leaders Better Schools. Now it's time to share why what we do works and serve more leaders at scale. I call our approach the ABCs of powerful professional development™. Leaders thrive in our community because of the authenticity, belonging, and challenge they experience. And I believe it will revolutionize how leaders are supported around the world.

In Chapter 2, I'll briefly introduce the model, share some general data that represent our community, and talk about the kind of leaders we serve. Then, in Part II, we will dive deeply into each component of the model. Part of my hope is to get you excited about what we offer. I also hope that it inspires you to create and search out professional development that expresses the ABCs of powerful professional development™ in order for you to grow as a leader.

Mastermind Case Study
Demetrius Ball
Principal at Iron Horse Middle School

"If you can keep your head when all about you are losing theirs and blaming it on you . . ."

–Rudyard Kipling, "If"

Tell us what you do and what your work typically entails.

I am a middle school principal who supports 46 certificated teachers, 23 classified staff members, and 1,045 students on a daily basis. I am responsible for helping develop our school vision and a community that supports liberty and justice for all, which leads to us meeting our school mission.

How has the mastermind helped you?

The mastermind has helped me develop into a competent and confident school leader. Actually, I probably would not be a building principal if it were not for being a member of the mastermind. I learned almost seven years ago (2014), as a classroom teacher working toward my administrative credential, that I could not wait for my school or district to prepare me to be an educational leader. That year I discovered what it meant to be a "connected educator" when I was introduced to EduTwitter. In 2015 I discovered Better Leaders Better Schools, and I actually think I reached out to Danny at the end of that year because his message resonated with me. When I found out about the mastermind, I was a bit hesitant because, like everyone else, my time was limited, but being a member of the mastermind has been time well invested. I have learned so many leadership lessons simply by studying our books, but the discussions and problem solving we do together gave me the confidence to apply for and acquire my first principal position.

What's the best part of the mastermind?

The best part of the mastermind is the "Hot Seat." The intro engagement activities that each member shares at the beginning of each meeting are invaluable. I take them and use them in every one of my staff meetings. The books and subsequent discussions are valuable as well by helping me understand leadership overall and school leadership specifically. Each of those components is top level, but the Hot Seat is the most valuable. Getting to hear about the challenges that school leaders from around the world are currently facing, and then being able to brainstorm through those situations is invaluable to my effectiveness as a school leader. We talk about personnel opportunities, career progressions, student and family concerns, establishing and eliminating systems, maintaining a balanced life, and

(Continued)

(Continued)

so many other practical experiences. The community that we build in the mastermind allows for every topic to be on the table for discussion.

What is one way the mastermind has helped you approach leadership differently?

The mastermind pushes me to see things from multiple perspectives. When we talk about topics, it is great to hear the thoughts of leaders who may take a completely different approach to solving a problem than me.

What advice would you give a leader considering joining the mastermind?

I will always give leaders considering joining the mastermind the same advice: This will be one of the best, if not the best, investment that you've ever made in yourself. Not only are we a professional development group, but most importantly, we're a family.

Chapter 1 Reflection Questions

How often are you participating in professional development that grows you?

Think about how your district is developing you. Are you satisfied with that experience? If your needs are being met, what is the district doing that you value? If your needs are not being met, make a plan to take your development into your own hands.

How isolated are you as a leader? What needs to change? What are you willing to do to connect with a network of leaders who will support your development?

Are you bringing your full self to work? To what extent are you able to ignore being the leader you *think* others want you to be, in order to be your authentic leadership self?

The Solution 2

//

"The mastermind has provided me with the most effective, long-lasting, and deep personal improvement I have ever encountered."

−Chris Jones, member of the "Guiding Principals" mastermind cohort

Mastermind Snapshot

A former wrestler with a magnificent beard, Chris Jones is a strong leader in both build and mindset. He is a principal at a large high school in Massachusetts and has been a member of the "Guiding Principals" mastermind cohort since 2017. We have presented together at national conferences, and I am indebted to Chris's championing of our leadership community over the years. I asked him to write about his experience within the mastermind and here is what he had to say:

"What I have been able to accomplish thanks to the mastermind is too far-reaching for an easy description. I became a member of the mastermind shortly after I had accepted a position as a high school principal. I had always searched out professional development to assist with my urge to continually improve, but up until this point I felt as if everywhere I turned for help was focused on shallow and short-term gains. It was while I sat and watched various presenters at the NASSP national conference that I decided I didn't want to just develop myself. I wanted to be

(Continued)

(Continued)

a leader who could develop others and who could have people look to me for help. I didn't know how that was going to occur, but I knew one thing; I needed to change how I was approaching leadership altogether if I was to accomplish what I hoped. After meeting and speaking with Danny, I had a feeling the mastermind was a place to start this transformation.

My transformation started with a relatively disorganized, unfocused individual who, while having a deep desire to continually improve, lacked the vision and deeper understanding of leadership to make it happen. While it is not complete (true transformations never really are) I find myself in a place where I am not just staring at ever greater accomplishments, but in possession of the people and tools that will help me get there.

My membership in the mastermind has provided me with the most effective, long-lasting, and deep personal improvement I have ever encountered. There are many ways I've grown, but three key areas that I have noticed the most change in are productivity, servant-leadership, and vision.

It has improved my productivity and organizational skills. I now practice a morning ritual every morning that gets me prepared for the day. I have created an ideal week that allows me, as some of my teachers have put it, 'to get more done than they could imagine.' I now get into classes and provide feedback every day while continuing to have consistent communication with the community. I read books outside of education and focus on different levels of those I serve as a leader.

The mastermind has fostered a perspective of serving others by providing support and resources. I am a self-proclaimed (and practicing) 'teacher-centered principal' because I know that the best way to serve the most students is by leveraging the ability of teachers to serve them. The mastermind has taught me to be a more engaging and authentic leader so that I am able to motivate staff through this lens.

All of these things that I have gained from the mastermind would mean less than they do without a vision to carry my work forward. With the focus on sustainable improvements through purposeful planning, I continuously work with my building leadership team on identifying and attaining long-range goals based on core values. I am now driven by decision-making connected to our larger 'why.' This has been successful because of what the mastermind has taught me concerning productivity, decision-making, and reflection. The mastermind is what every leader who is serious about making a lasting impact needs; the opportunity to be part of a supportive group of innovative leaders who question the norm, push each other to be better for others, and offer support throughout the journey of wins and losses.

If one is looking for tangible results of the mastermind, I have those as well. I now regularly present at state-level conferences and have presented at three national conferences. I have been on multiple podcasts (stemming from my first Better Leaders Better Schools *appearance) and am in the midst of authoring a book. I serve on multiple state association committees and have created numerous creative, long-lasting school programs to increase all students' success. I continue to foster the creation of other leaders in my organization. I have improved as a person because the mastermind is not about a singular focus on leadership. It is about developing individuals as a whole so they can become better leaders"* (Jones, personal communication, October 27, 2020).

Chris has experienced tremendous transformation and growth in the mastermind. That type of development is the promise we make to each and every member. In this chapter, you'll learn a little more about what the mastermind looks like from a high level, and through Part II of this book, we'll dig into specifically what makes it a powerful professional development experience. Now that we've looked at Chris's story, let's take a look at mastermind members as a whole.

Our Community

The mastermind currently has 60 members, and you might find the demographics of our community interesting:

- 55 percent are male

- 45 percent are female

- 26 percent are leaders of color

- 50 percent are principals

- 17 percent are assistant principals

- 16 percent are central office leaders

- 16 percent are instructional coaches or deans

Our members are "Ruckus Makers," which I define as "out-of-the-box leaders who make change happen in education."[23] Later in this chapter I will introduce a "mindset scorecard" that illustrates the kind of leaders we love to serve in the mastermind.

Lizzy, an American citizen leading a Nepalese school, connects with the idea of being a Ruckus Maker. It attracted her to the group. In fact, she connected with this message I sent her via email:

> If you have ever thought, "Am I crazy?" because your dreams and vision for education are so innovative and bold, then we have a community of leaders just like you.

---

[23] It's time for another giveaway. We have some great Ruckus Maker swag at the Better Leaders Better Schools store. Be the first reader to post a *video* review of this book and I'll send you a shirt or a hat (or maybe both). Send your video review and a link to where you posted your review to daniel@betterleadersbetterschools.com to get your swag.

You're not crazy.

You're a Ruckus Maker making a difference. (Bauer, personal communication, May 12, 2020)

Lizzy responded to this communication this way:

> This is what sets your brand apart from everyone else. It's not just about mastery of principles or systems, feedback conversations, or social skills as a leader—which are all important! It's about pushing the envelope, finding others who are doing the same, and becoming a better leader by working on the whole package of who you are. It's a place for outliers and risk-takers. (Neiger, personal communication, May 12, 2020)

Thank you, Lizzy, I couldn't have said it better myself!

This is our community. Thought leaders have been calling for disruption in education for a long time. In 2020, COVID-19 and the reality of systemic racism disrupted education whether it was ready or not.[24] The Better Leaders Better Schools mastermind is designed to connect innovative leaders who are willing to take risks that make education better. Speaking of innovative leaders, let's look at the characteristics and mindsets of ideal mastermind members next.

/////////////////////////////

The Better Leaders Better Schools mastermind is designed to connect innovative leaders who are willing to take risks that make education better.

---

[24] We were ready. Since 2016 the mastermind had been connecting on Zoom, so each member felt comfortable switching to a hybrid and virtual setting. It wasn't easy, but our leaders were prepared. We also talk about tough issues—including equity and racism—and our members are creating schools that are welcoming environments and beacons of compassion in their communities.

The Ideal Member

Leadership Mindset

According to Duke (2019, pp. 78–84), we make decisions based on what we believe, which leads to either a positive or a negative outcome. Leaders also struggle to separate the quality of a decision from the outcome. It is much easier to say we made a bad decision when the outcome is also poor. Unfortunately, that is rarely the case. Leaders can make great decisions that lead to a negative outcome, and this happens more frequently than we want to acknowledge. Another wrinkle is that many outcomes are completely out of our control. Can a school leader really move the needle on attendance, discipline, and achievement? Of course they can with a great amount of skill, but we must not forget that so many of our outcomes are out of our direct control and, in reality, are influenced by luck.

I agree that our beliefs are what drive our actions and inform our decisions. When I consider the kinds of leaders who have joined the mastermind, I look for the commonalities when it comes to beliefs, which I call mindset.

> Getting it together mentally . . . involves the learning of several internal skills: 1) learning how to get the clearest possible picture of your desired outcomes; 2) learning how to trust [yourself] to perform . . . and learn from both successes and failures; 3) learning to see "nonjudgmentally"—that is, to see what is happening rather than merely noticing how well or how badly it is happening. This overcomes "trying too hard." All these skills are subsidiary to the master skill, without which nothing of value is ever achieved: the art of relaxed concentration. (Gallwey, 1975/2015, p. 13)

There are twelve mindsets that mastermind members share. First, I will describe in detail what these mindsets are and then I will share a tool we call the "mindset scorecard."[25] This tool is invaluable in that it breaks down each mindset across a continuum of 1–12 points for each mindset. What also makes the scorecard helpful is that leaders can score where they currently are in relation to each mindset and where they want to go. The tension produced by looking at the gap between present and future opens a discussion and path forward for leaders to take in their professional growth. Later, in Chapter 5, we will look at the scorecard again to explore how we use it to challenge our members and filter applicants to our community.

The Ideal Leader

Not everyone is going to have a seat on the bus. There is definitely an ideal leader who we want to join our community. Our ideal member is a Ruckus Maker—an out-of-the-box leader who makes change happen in education. But in addition to this foundational posture, an ideal mastermind member also exemplifies the following mindset qualities.

Generous. It's very important that leaders in our community have a generous spirit. School leaders apply to the mastermind regularly, and the next step is basically an interview. The school leader wants to answer, "Is the mastermind the right professional development opportunity for me?" At the same time, I wonder, "Will this leader add value to our community?" From time to time, I meet a leader with the wrong point of view. They are only interested in what the mastermind is going to

---

[25] I learned to develop a mindset scorecard from Dan Sullivan, who runs Strategic Coach®, an organization that provides business coaching for growth-minded entrepreneurs.

do for them. The value of joining a global network of innovative school leaders should be clear. What I look for in an ideal candidate is that they are showing up ready to give. They know that by adding value to the community, the rest will take care of itself and whatever way they are looking to develop will come back to them if they focus on serving first.

Hunger. This equates to a *desire to learn* and a *hunger to level up.* Some leaders tell me either they don't read or they don't have time for it. That is a warning flag to me. Harry S Truman said, "Not all readers are leaders, but all leaders are readers." Time and again, mastermind members thank me for the books we read and other materials I share that help them grow. Reading doesn't have to be the main mode. I know there are different ways people like to learn. It is integral that our mastermind members have a strong desire to continue to grow. Staying stagnant is not an option.

Wanting to develop their skills or grow their capacity usually follows a strong desire to learn. The reason why isn't as important to me, but all of our community members know that they can have a greater impact in the world, and the way to get there is to level up their skill set. Top performers are keenly aware of what is in their control, and one of the most leverageable actions a leader can take is to get better. Comfortable leaders should not apply to our community, which brings us to the next point on feedback.

Welcomes Feedback. One of the best ways to develop your leadership capacity is through candid feedback loops. Some leaders don't want honest feedback. This is where the idea of a "yes" man or woman comes into play. A choice every leader makes is who they surround themselves with. The most effective leaders build a team that pushes back on ideas to make them better as well as shares what TJ Vari and Joseph Jones call *candid and compassionate feedback.* This kind of feedback is aimed at helping an individual grow, but at times it may sting like a good workout. At the time it may not feel great, but we know that in the end it will make us better.

Candid. If you want to pretend how great you are, then spend more time on social media and tell the world. What we are looking for in the mastermind are leaders who can be candid with themselves and with other members. It's important to be honest with ourselves so that we can identify how and why we want to grow. It's also important so that we aren't choosing to live with blind spots. Candor is valuable when providing feedback to others as well. I call this "spinach in your teeth" behavior. If we were out to eat and I had spinach in my teeth, I would want you to tell me. Mastermind members are the ones who break through uncomfortable silence to say what needs to be said in order to be helpful.

Open-minded. One main reason leaders join the mastermind is that they are aware of the groupthink that exists within their district and they want to expose themselves to new ideas. Whether it is the financial corruption of a company like Enron, or the way Volkswagen cheated emissions tests in order to sell more cars, cultures do exist in a bubble—even positive ones. A great way to become a better leader is to network with other leaders who do things differently, maybe even better. By exposing themselves to new ideas weekly, mastermind members bring a fresh perspective back to their bubbles and show different ways of making education better.

Collaborative. There is an African proverb that says, "If you want to go fast, go alone. If you want to go far, go together." The mastermind is communal. We believe that all of us are better than any of us. Leading in isolation is a choice and the greatest enemy of excellence. Our members know that the smartest person in the room is the collective wisdom of the room itself. Ideal mastermind members want to collaborate because they know that in order to be their best, they can't operate alone.

Excellence. We don't work with leaders on a professional improvement plan. That is an edge we chose. Steve Jobs said that A players want to be around other A players. Surrounding A players with B- or C-quality individuals is a sure-fire way to demotivate high-performing leaders. If you do this, they will leave. We want high-performing school leaders in our community who will push each other to be remarkable. We want our community to feel different from what leaders may experience in their home districts. One superintendent told me that he paid for one principal's membership because that leader had maximized every leadership development opportunity available within the district. Like a great teacher, this superintendent differentiated how he offered professional development to his top principals, and they have thrived in our community.

Antiracist. I wish this was common sense, but it's not. Our community works diligently to dismantle white supremacy culture and systemic racism within the schools our members lead. Our country is diverse, and we will meet the needs of all students by creating safe, supportive, and compassionate environments that offer a culturally relevant and authentic learning experience.

Emotional Intelligence. We want leaders who are internally and externally aware. This is a baseline requirement to participate in our community because emotionally unintelligent leaders are toxic and harm cultures by choice or unintentionally. We have created a special place and protect that by bringing in the right kind of leaders.

Ownership. Individuals who say "I accept no responsibility" are leaders in title only. Mastermind members
work hard at sharing everything, warts and all, because
they value critical feedback that will push them to be
better. Part of that is accepting responsibility for mistakes made. In the context of restorative practices, we
talk about the harm that is caused as a result of our
choices. Part of taking ownership is repairing relationships when harm is caused. Another way to accept
responsibility is to be candid with yourself, reflecting on
the errors made during the day. You can ask yourself two
helpful questions: What could I have changed to make
my day better? and What did I learn from the mistakes
I made today? The Stoic, Epictetus, recommended at the
end of every day to meditate on these questions:

Let not sleep descend on your weary eyes

Before having reviewed every action of the day.

*Where did I go wrong? What did I do? What duty to
leave undone?*

Starting here, review your actions, and afterward,

*Blame yourself for what is badly done, and rejoice in
the good (Epictetus, ca. 108/2014, p. 163).*

It's not a matter of whether we are going to make
mistakes each day; what matters is what we learn
from them.

Another part of taking ownership is being *solutions-
focused.* The mastermind is not the faculty lounge, nor
is it a private social media group. A pet peeve of mine
is people who complain. Discussing what is wrong is
easy to do; it's much harder to be a person of action and
one who is solution-focused. That doesn't mean that
our members don't get upset and need time to vent.
We create a safe space within the mastermind where

everyone can be themselves 100 percent, but with every discussion of transgression we want to move quickly to what we can do about it. Many things are out of control. Those that fall outside our influence we need to let go of fully. What is in our control is where our focus then turns and we commit to working to find a solution.

Goals. It's amazing to me how many leaders haven't taken the time to create precise goals that meaningfully inform and direct their work each and every day. Many leaders we support through the mastermind do have goals, but allow the "tyranny of the urgent" and other obstacles to sidetrack their ability to follow through on these goals. We help leaders move from that place of frustration to one of focus. Goals should be priorities, and everything else other than a true subset of actual, predetermined emergencies can wait.

Compassion. Top performers integrate their personal and professional lives. It is a myth that leaders should not mix the personal and professional, and it is counterproductive to do so. Every human being is a complex and beautiful creature. What happens outside of work influences the *actual* work we do. There is no denying that, and leaders who don't recognize this aren't operating in reality. Worse, your staff *wants* to connect with you. That doesn't mean you are friends with everyone outside of school, but it does mean that your staff knows you care. By building relational capital, the staff you serve will be willing to run through a wall for you, not out of blind obedience but because they care about you and the mission of the school. Theodore Roosevelt's saying, "People don't care how much you know until they know how much you care," is helpful here.

The Mindset Scorecard

Figure 2.1 shows the mindset scorecard. After a leader applies to join our mastermind, I ask them to complete this scorecard to get a sense of where they are in their leadership. There is no "right" score that guarantees a leader is approved for membership. What I love about this tool is that not only is it robust, but it includes a present versus future component. This allows the leader to reflect on where they are currently and where they want to go. It also helps me understand where a leader sees themself, and what we can work on through the mastermind to improve their mindset.[26] We'll revisit the mastermind scorecard again in Chapter 5.

The Application

One tool I use to filter potential mastermind members is the application. It's a short process that takes about nine minutes to complete. Like the mindset scorecard, I use this tool to challenge leaders to reflect on where they are as a leader. I also want to slow the process down and cause some friction for a leader to join. By slowing the process down, leaders who want to plug into the mastermind experience continue, and those who give up obviously aren't prioritizing their leadership development. For example, Bill Renner joined the mastermind in 2021 after hearing about it for four years. Since 2016, Bill knew this was the professional development experience he was looking for, but the timing wasn't right. His wife is a working professional, and his kids were at an age that they needed adult supervision after school hours. Four years later, his kids were old enough to experience some more independence and the timing was right for Bill and his wife. During our strategy call, Bill told me more about the mastermind than any other leader I've spoken with on an exploratory call. He had done his homework, and

---

[26] I also challenge you, Dear Reader, to complete this scorecard and share your results with mastermind@betterleadersbetterschools. com. Someone on my team will reach out and offer a complimentary coaching call to help you develop a plan to improve your leadership mindset.

Figure 2.1   Mastermind Mindset Scorecard

	1 2 3	4 5 6	7 8 9	10 11 12	NOW	NEXT
GENEROUS	You are a taker. Sharing resources is scary. You see the world in terms of scarcity.	You are a taker who sometimes gives when the outcome of generosity benefits you. You believe, "I'll scratch your back if you scratch mine."	You are a giver. Generosity comes naturally, but at a cost when you violate personal boundaries in order to help. This zaps your energy and ability to have more impact.	You see abundance everywhere. Generosity comes naturally and you look for ways to share resources. You honor individual boundaries so that you can be even more generous at appropriate times.		
HUNGER	You engage in professional development only when directed. You don't see value in opportunities that others find meaningful. You judge your peers' motives for seeking professional development.	You say "No" too easily to growth opportunities. Obstacles block you from professional development rather than opportunities to navigate around.	You invest in opportunities that require minimal resources. Social media, podcasts, & free workshops are enough for you. A lack of prioritizing your growth is hindering your ability to maximize your performance.	You search for the best growth experiences. You find creative solutions to enroll in programs you identify as worthy of investment. What fuels you is a desire to be the best version of yourself.		
WELCOMES FEEDBACK	You avoid feedback and discount the value of feedback shared with you.	You take action on feedback, but discount the value of feedback based on the messenger.	You actively seek out feedback and have developed great trust with peers who have permission to challenge you to be better.	You deliberately consider feedback and use systems to learn from both positive and negative outcomes. You have access to multiple feedback loops. You share what you are learning with your peers.		
CANDID	Your message changes based on the environment and people around. You talk out of both sides of your mouth.	You demonstrate candor with a small group of peers who are in your comfort zone.	You care personally & challenge directly but struggle to implement consistently.	You consistently care personally and challenge directly.		
OPEN-MINDED	The world is black and white. You believe you are either right or wrong. You don't interact with peers who don't share your point-of-view.	The world is black and white, but you are willing to work with others who don't share your perspective.	You see the world as more than black and white. However, you lack intentional tools to gather diverse opinions and slow your thinking down.	You demonstrate curiosity in every situation and use tools to slow your thinking and suspend judgment. You demonstrate empathy and seek out counter-narratives to balance your thinking.		
COLLABORATIVE	You work in isolation.	You collaborate when asked, but you don't actively seek collaboration.	You value collaboration and gathering people comes naturally. The groups you form are homogeneous.	You value collaboration and gathering people comes naturally. You are able to gather diverse groups of people.		
EXCELLENCE	Your work is consistently poor.	You can create excellent work with great effort. This output is inconsistent.	You do all things with excellence. This comes at a cost because you are not able to let some things go. It's hard to separate the forest from the trees.	Your goal is to do everything with excellence. You have a pre-determined list of items that must be done with excellence and are able to let go of tasks that don't matter in the "big picture."		

ANTIRACIST	You are racist.	You are willing to acknowledge that racism exists, but for you it exists in the past or in other spaces. You are unwilling to admit that racism exists where you are.	You are self-aware and see where your actions contribute to inequity. You actively seek out ways to grow and understand others from different backgrounds. You speak up inconsistently when you experience something racist.	You are self-aware and see where your actions contribute to inequity. You actively seek out ways to grow and understand others from different backgrounds. You speak up consistently when you experience something racist.
EMOTIONAL INTELLIGENCE	When people ask who the "jerk" is in the organization, everyone says it is you.	You have either strong internal or external awareness, but you are not working at growing either of these areas.	You have either strong internal or external awareness. You actively work at strengthening your emotional intelligence.	You have both strong internal and external awareness. You actively work at strengthening your emotional intelligence. Peers come to you to learn how to grow in this area.
OWNERSHIP	It is always someone else's fault.	You take responsibility when you are uncomfortable or forced to take responsibility because someone of authority makes you.	You take ownership when you are at fault and can do so unprompted.	You take ownership in all situations. Even when someone else is clearly at fault, you are able to iden- tify where you either contributed to the problem or where you could have done something better.
GOALS	You lack authentic goals. If you have them at all they are done to fulfill compliance, but lack meaning for your work.	You have goals, but they are created to please others. They are what you think your boss, peers, or others you respect would want you to have.	You have clearly defined goals and work toward them. The tyranny of the urgent sidetracks your goals and you lose focus.	You have clearly defined and written goals. You share your goals and progress in public. You are able to teach others how to set and achieve goals. You demonstrate focus and urgent needs don't sidetrack what is most important.
COMPASSION	People describe you as cold and mean.	You believe the professional and personal must be separate. There is a palpable distance between you and colleagues.	You are compassionate and bring your full self to work. However, you don't consistently share tough feedback because you care so much for others. Because of this, your motives are sometimes questioned.	You are warm and compassionate. People "know how much you care" and are open to your ideas. Because of your high regard for others you can share tough feedback. You integrate your personal and professional lives appropriately. People feel seen, heard, and connected because of your leadership.
			COMPASSION	0	0

for him, joining the mastermind was a slow and deliberate process. This also means that when he eventually decided to join, he was "all in."

On the application, I ask for contact information and in which group a leader is interested. I won't share those here in the book. The following are the long-form questions I use on the application to get to know the applicant and a brief explanation of why I use them.

Where are you going? Tell us about your goals over the next year. As I mentioned in the mindset section prior to this, a shocking number of leaders do not have concrete goals that guide their yearly, quarterly, monthly, weekly, and daily work. Seneca said, "If one does not know to which port one is sailing, no wind is favorable." This quote is usually used in reference to vision, and goals are a derivative of vision. The other common challenge I see is that leaders have, in fact, identified concrete goals, but they allow other people's priorities and emergencies to pull them away from what they've determined as most important. There are a variety of reasons for the lack of focus and execution. This section gives me a sense of what applicants to the mastermind have set out to achieve. It also shows me how big (or small) they are playing in terms of goals.

Leaders join the mastermind to level up. Tell us about a time of significant personal growth. Why are you looking to grow right now? This question helps me understand what leaders have done to inspire growth in the past. I also learn how invested they are in their growth. Attending an annual conference is one thing. Investing in a nine-day leadership intensive is quite another. This question also helps me see from the applicants' point of view what they consider growth and how they have been developing themselves over the years.

During the "hot seat" in the mastermind meeting, leaders help each other solve significant challenges. What challenge(s) do you face and could you use support with currently? These challenges can be real or perceived. The obstacles question gives me a hint of how we need to serve this leader in the mastermind and if there is an opportunity for any quick wins. Alex identified the following as the obstacles on his leadership journey:

> "We are a high-performing school but with little, to no, *intentional* processes. It is hard to get movement out of people who have consistently been a part of one of the top schools in the state but the cycle of continuous improvement has to begin so that we can reach even greater heights. I am the lone administrator in the building (along with a full-time counselor) so the weight of instructional leadership falls squarely on my shoulders. This requires me to hone my skills to an even greater level because we have so few areas of glaring weakness as a school. I am trying to navigate taking a good school to a great school and feel isolated in the process."

When considering your application, is there anything else you'd like us to know? This is actually my favorite question. Many leaders use this open-ended question to tell me more about their professional experience, but I absolutely love it when an applicant shares something personal or, better yet, creative that I'm not expecting.

(Continued)

(Continued)

This is a great way for a leader to set themselves apart from other potential mastermind members.

If you're thinking about starting a mastermind and choose to use an application, consider what you might ask. The purpose of mine is to build a small hoop to jump through that can act as a filter for potential members. Since the most important questions are open-ended, I can see if some of our values come through in the application. From here I invite the applicant to a 30-minute exploratory call to decide on whether or not to offer the leader a seat at our table in the mastermind. I'll explain that next.

Why do you want to join the mastermind?
Everyone has a reason. This tells me what they see as the value of what our community offers. Here is how Brandon answers this question:

> "Building administration is a lonely gig, and I don't want to accept that as 'what it is.' I want to be my best as a school leader because I have great staff and great kids, both in need of a lot of support. I also need to be my best as a dad, and I often feel like putting what I do into the school pulls me away (both physically and mentally). What better way to hit all of these issues than to be in touch with peers who are living it or have lived it? There are too many people out there crushing this game for me to travel this journey alone!"

What I like about Brandon's response is that he is clearly hungry and knows there is a "better way" of leading in a community versus isolation.

The Model

Everyone Wins When a Leader Gets Better.
Everyone Wins When You Get Better.

Years ago Simon Sinek created a TED talk that went viral—this was his famous "Start with the Why" or Golden Circle talk. The idea is simple yet profound. According to Sinek, organizations have it all wrong. Instead of leading with what they offer—the service, product, or widget, they should instead lead with the why. Schools should do the same. Of course, all schools want all students to achieve at a high level and become responsible members of society, but what is the why that drives it all?

The logic behind Sinek's talk is that people don't care about what you do or what you offer. Instead, they care about why you are doing it, how you are doing it, and then what you actually do. In the TED talk, Sinek uses the example of Apple.

Apple's why: Everything we do, we believe in challenging the status quo, we believe in thinking differently.

Apple's how: We make products that are beautifully designed and user-friendly.

Apple's what: We just happen to make great computers—do you want to buy one?

I cannot emphasize enough how important the golden circle is to organizational life and success. It is what has propelled the mastermind and the work done at Better Leaders Better Schools. Take time to think deeply about the why-how-what of your work if you want your staff to own the vision and make it a reality. It works for Apple. It has worked for us at Better Leaders Better Schools, and it will work for you.

Our why: We believe, "Everyone wins when a leader gets better. Everyone wins when you get better."

Our how: We do this through creating an environment where leaders can be authentic, experience belonging, and be challenged to grow.

Our what: We call this leadership community "the mastermind." Do you want to join?

I share these examples so that you can apply them to your leadership and organization. The golden circle can also act as a filter when evaluating what professional development opportunities to create. The "what" of professional development is easy to see: books, online summits, in-person conferences, PLCs, individual coaches, and so on. The "what" is also easy to offer. The "why" and the "how" separate experiences and communicate how they are different with intentionality.

Now that we know the golden circle for Better Leaders Better Schools, let's take a look at the ABCs of powerful professional development™.

Chapter 1 discussed many of the ways that professional development comes up short, the problem of isolation in school leadership, and many of the opportunities missed in districts each day. Although these professional development ills are prevalent, they don't have to be permanent. Creating powerful professional development is as simple as ABC (Figure 2.2); this is how I built the mastermind at Better Leaders Better Schools. A stands for authenticity; B represents belonging; and C is for challenge. In my experience, putting together all these components leads to personal and professional transformation in a school leader's life.

Authenticity + Belonging + Challenge = Transformation

Figure 2.2   The ABCs of Powerful Professional
Development™

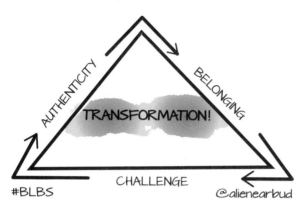

In Part II, we will look at why these ABCs lead to a transformational experience for school leaders. Authenticity
matters because leaders need a place where they can be
themselves, without judgment. In this kind of environment they can freely admit what they don't know and ask
for help. They can also celebrate their wins without worrying others will think they are an egomaniac. Belonging
is central to powerful professional development as well.
One of the most common challenges a school leader
faces is isolation. That can be due to a myriad of reasons,
so providing a space where people feel accepted, connected, seen, and heard is invaluable. It's like the Bull
and Finch Pub.[27] Finally, leaders want to grow. They want
to be challenged and pushed to take their skills to the

---

[27] The Bull and Finch Pub was the inspiration for the popular
American sitcom called *Cheers*. This show ran for eleven years
from 1982–1993. The theme song was titled, "Where Everyone
Knows Your Name" and illustrates the importance of belonging.
In my lifetime, various churches, my fraternity in college, the
gym where I worked out, local coffee shops, and a local water-
ing hole have all served as places that provided relationships and
community for me.

next level. Just like Galileo's theory of relativity, leaders who join the mastermind do so because they know that inaction—staying in place—is actually regression. If they aren't growing, they are regressing. If everyone wins when you get better, you owe it to your community to develop yourself as much as possible.

Districts can encourage leaders to keep progressing by providing the resources and committing to their development.

Greatest Investments

Leadership development is worth a district's investment of time and financial resources. Leaders who participate in leadership training improve their leadership versus those who do not (Tafvelin et al., 2019, p. 34). The idea that leaders grow when engaging in leadership training seems like common sense, and it is. Unfortunately, it is not common practice.

My lived experience as a local school leader taught this to me. I experienced "leadership" meetings to be bureaucratic boredom sessions focused on attendance, discipline, and student achievement rather than the real work of a leader (e.g., crafting a meaningful vision, navigating difficult conversations, or dismantling systemic racism within the school).

So when the district didn't provide leadership training, I created my own path in 2015 by launching the *Better Leaders Better Schools* podcast. I figured if I learned from the successes and failures of other leaders, and took action on just one idea, then my leadership skills would grow. This proved to be true over hundreds of episodes and millions of downloads later.

Transformational leadership theory teaches us that leadership training influences leadership behavior in countless ways. Leaders are able to reframe stressful situations and see them as opportunities for growth; they replace the feeling of isolation with one of connectedness, and they learn to listen carefully and respond to the needs of their staff (Tafvelin et al., 2019, p. 35). The mastermind is a great return on investment, and in this chapter, you have gotten a taste of what the mastermind is about and the model it is built on. Later, in Part II, we will dive deep into how professional development can include authenticity, belonging, and challenge in each experience.

When professional development is built on the ABCs, it leads to transformation. The rest of Part II will look at ways we make the mastermind an experience where leaders can be authentic, belong, get challenged, and ultimately transform. It is my hope that these ideas come across clearly so that you can apply them to professional development you facilitate and use them as a tool to evaluate future experiences you choose to invest in.

Mastermind Case Study

Chris Horton
Principal in British Columbia, Canada

How many professional development events, conferences, or activities have had a long-term, powerful impact on your leadership or practice?

(Continued)

(Continued)

Based on my own experiences with professional development, I would guess very few. The ones that have had a lasting impact on my thinking and my practice all involved an ongoing connection to and accountability with a group of peers. I have always loved the energy, ideas, and ways of thinking that you hear at conferences and other one-off professional development. They can be inspiring, but they often turn into little action. For some who have that unique skill to take information/ideas and move them to action, they can be impactful. In many respects, when it comes to professional growth, that's not me.

Early in my administration career, I had the privilege to be involved in some professional learning that involved regular connections with a small group of three other school leaders to practice skills, hold each other accountable, and have professional conversations. After I completed these trainings, I realized the importance of the regular connection and relationship that is found in ongoing, continuous forms of professional learning. The timing of my discovery of the BLBS mastermind could not have been better.

The discovery of the mastermind was entirely by accident. I was surfing the internet looking for some ideas about some leadership topic, I don't even remember what it was exactly now. As I was searching, I came across this website called Better Leaders Better Schools. The title alone resonated with me. I wanted to be a better leader so that my school could be better. I spent time exploring the website and finding resources, and I started listening to the *Better Leaders Better Schools* podcast on my commute. As I listened to the podcast, Danny started mentioning this thing called the mastermind. His description intrigued me because it aligned with these previous powerful professional learning opportunities I had been involved in. I read more about it on the website, then reached out to Danny. I started in a group shortly after that. I have now been a member of a mastermind group for more than three years.

As I reflect on what the mastermind has meant to me and to my leadership, it is quite emotional. The mastermind took me from a young, immature leader to a more mature leader who has confidence in my leadership, my values, my beliefs, and my vision for learning. It was through the incredibly rich conversations with school leaders from a wide variety of walks of life, parts of the world, and experiences that this occurred. Every week, even when I'm not on the hot seat, I'm learning how to approach challenges, celebrate victories, and raise the bar on my own leadership. The mastermind has become a second family that I miss deeply when I am unable to attend even for a single week. They are my cheerleaders, my mentors, and my support system. I know that each of us would bend over backward to support another member through leadership and personal challenges. All this, and most of us have never even met in person. All this, and we also have Danny, our "fearless leader." He would never say he is our leader, but without him, none of this would be real. His passion for learning and leading, his humility, and his quiet (well, not always quiet) leadership serve as a foundation that makes the mastermind what it is to each of us. He continues to push all of us, provide sound advice, ask great questions, and push himself in his own leadership journey—a true mentor and role model.

I will never be the same, thank goodness, as a result of the mastermind and Danny Bauer. It brings tears of gratitude and joy to my eyes as I write this. I have been profoundly impacted and changed by this experience. I look forward to the next three (and hopefully more) years and what they will bring in my leadership and my life as I continue to engage in the mastermind. And I can't wait to meet everyone in person, to run up to them and give them a huge hug. They are, after all, my leadership family.

Chapter 2 Reflection Questions

Think about the best professional development you have experienced. What made it work for you?

Look at the mindset scorecard and evaluate yourself. Where are you now? Where would you like to be in the future?[28]

Consider creating a mindset scorecard for your ideal staff member, student, and parent. If you accepted this challenge, how would you adapt what's on our scorecard for the purposes of your school?

What about the ABCs of powerful professional development™ do you relate to? Where do you see authenticity, belonging, and challenge show up in the professional development you experience? How do you integrate these components in your school or district?

---

[28] As I mentioned earlier in this chapter, if you would benefit from a powerful coaching conversation on the mindset scorecard with a Better Leaders Better Schools expert coach, reach out to mastermind@betterleadersbetterschools.com and we'll follow up with how to set that up.

Part II

When thinking about why the mastermind works so well and what makes it a powerful professional development opportunity, I was able to identify authenticity, belonging, and challenge as the foundational aspects that lead to transformation.

In Part II, we will dive deep into the ABCs and look at each component from another three angles. Authenticity is made up of safety, self-awareness, and being values-driven. Belonging is fueled by a shared purpose, inclusive environment, and trust. Challenge is established through leadership mindset, taking action, and creating a powerful community.

I acknowledge that there can be some overlap. One example could be how an idea in the authenticity/self-awareness section could easily fit into the mindset/challenge section. Another example is how psychological safety allows leaders to experience authenticity, but it also connects us and fosters belonging. These section titles are useful for the reader in terms of understanding the model, but like any worthwhile experience, there is fluidity between the components. In some respects the model represents an infinitely generative experience like autocatalysis, where the lighting of the initial spark provides enough energy to keep the momentum moving forward in an infinite loop. I like to think of the mastermind in these terms because it reflects the "ripple effect" I've seen and members have experienced within our community. As we grow, we take what we've learned to make the communities we serve even better. The reciprocity

Authenticity is made up of safety, self-awareness, and being values-driven. Belonging is fueled by a shared purpose, inclusive environment, and trust. Challenge is established through leadership mindset, taking action, and creating a powerful community.

demonstrated and shared continues to build on each other. It helps us live out the idea that "everyone wins when a leader gets better. Everyone wins when you get better."

Part II will show you the exact components of how we make that happen each week in the mastermind.

Authenticity 3

Safety

I wish I could show you,

When you are lonely or in darkness,

The Astonishing Light

Of your own Being!

—Hafiz, "My Brilliant Image"

In 2015, Google released the results of a two-year study in which their People Operations team conducted 200+ interviews with their employees to find out what makes their teams effective. They looked at more than 250 attributes of 180+ Google teams. The results were surprising. They thought they would find the importance of key personnel, "super stars," but in reality *how* the team members interacted with each other was far more important than *who* made up the team. At the top of their list of effective teams was *psychological safety*, and they define this term as "Team members feel safe to take risks and be vulnerable in front of each other" (Rozovsky, 2015).

In Part I, we looked at the problems that limit the effectiveness of professional development. I argue that inauthenticity is one of those major factors. Inauthentic spaces squelch psychological safety. But for a team to truly soar and for professional development to be authentic and nurture the development of its leaders, it is essential that individuals feel comfortable enough to admit what they don't know and ask for help when needed.

Imagine that a leader doesn't ask for clarification at the onset of a project. Maybe because they were hesitant, afraid, or unconfident about their own contribution or approach. Then, they work for weeks working on the project, driven by incorrect assumptions that could have been clarified at the beginning of the project. Because of a lack of psychological safety, where would this project end up? "In the garbage" is a reasonable answer.

A lack of psychological safety means a lack of understanding and ultimately impact. When it comes to professional development, how much will a leader learn, digest, and ultimately embody if the experience is shared in an unsafe environment?

James Clear (2018), the author of *Atomic Habits*, uses a useful metaphor that shows the importance of psychological safety. He writes, "Imagine you are flying from Los Angeles to New York City. If a pilot leaving from LAX adjusts the heading just 3.5 degrees south, you will land in Washington, D.C., instead of New York" (p. 17). DC versus New York City is quite a distance apart! When leaders experience inauthentic and unsafe professional development, they go through the motions without asking for clarification. After leaving that professional development, they end up in Washington, DC versus New York City. The stakes of education and what we owe to our communities as school leaders are far too great to allow an error like this to happen in schools and districts around the world.

Safety is a foundational aspect of the mastermind and the authentic component of our operating model. There are a number of ways we do this in the mastermind, and we'll spend the rest of this chapter looking at how we do exactly that.

How Do You Build Psychological Safety?

In a deep dive into psychological safety, two studies are often cited: Google's 2015 Project Aristotle study on team effectiveness, and Amy Edmondson's 1999 study that defined the term *psychological safety*.

Edmondson (1999) defines psychological safety as

> a shared belief that the team is safe for interpersonal risk taking. For the most part, this belief tends to be tacit—taken for granted and not given direct attention, either by individuals or by the team as a whole. Although tacit beliefs about interpersonal norms are sometimes explicitly discussed in a team, their being made explicit does not alter the essence of team psychological safety. (p. 354)

Edmondson (1999) also identified the beliefs, behaviors, and constructs that fostered psychological safety in teams. Knowing these helps designers of professional development intentionally build safety into the experience. The beliefs are respect for peers' abilities, a genuine interest in each other as people, an environment that welcomes your thoughts, and a shared belief of positive intentions. The behaviors are seeking or giving feedback, and making changes and improvements (versus avoiding change or sticking with the status quo). The constructs are obtaining or providing help or expertise, experimenting, and engaging in constructive conflict or confrontation (pp. 360–361).

In the remainder of this section on psychological safety, we'll look at how we use the beliefs, behaviors, and constructs Edmondson (1999) suggests within the mastermind specifically. Table 3.1 previews practical activities and identifies where they align with the Edmondson model. After Table 3.1, we'll look at how to facilitate each activity.

Table 3.1   Activities That Build Psychological Safety in the Mastermind

ACTIVITY	HOW DOES IT BUILD PSYCHOLOGICAL SAFETY?
Check-in questions	• A genuine interest in peers • An environment that welcomes your thoughts
How are you feeling right now?	• A genuine interest in peers • An environment that welcomes your thoughts
Reflection questions	• A genuine interest in peers • An environment that welcomes your thoughts
Draw a peer	• Experimenting
What do you have in common?	• A genuine interest in peers • An environment that welcomes your thoughts
Imaginary gifts	• Experimenting
Name it	• Experimenting
Nicknames	• A genuine interest in peers
When you were ten years old	• A genuine interest in peers
Permission slips	• An environment that welcomes your thoughts
Wins-of-the-week	• Respect in peers' abilities • A genuine interest in peers
Silence	• An environment that welcomes your thoughts

Agreements	• An environment that welcomes your thoughts • A shared belief of positive intentions • Making changes and improvements
The One Big Thing	• Respect in peers' abilities • A genuine interest in peers • Making changes and improvements
Small groups	• A genuine interest in peers • An environment that welcomes your thoughts • Seeking or giving feedback • Making changes and improvements • Obtaining or providing help or expertise • Engaging in constructive conflict or confrontation
Hot seat	• Respect in peers' abilities • A genuine interest in peers • An environment that welcomes your thoughts • Seeking or giving feedback • Making changes and improvements • Obtaining or providing help or expertise • Engaging in constructive conflict or confrontation
Rotating facilitators	• Respect in peers' abilities • Seeking or giving feedback • Obtaining or providing help or expertise • Experimenting
Brainwriting	• Respect in peers' abilities • A genuine interest in peers • An environment that welcomes your thoughts
Donut pals	• Respect in peers' abilities • A genuine interest in peers • An environment that welcomes your thoughts • Making changes and improvements • Obtaining or providing help or expertise • Experimenting

Opening Activities

Check-in questions:

- In one sentence, what's it like to be you right now?

- 1–10 how are you right now? (1 = low 10 = high)

- What made you smile this week?

- What did you do that was scary this past week?

- How did you take a risk this week? What did you learn?[29]

How are you feeling right now? One of the main functions of the mastermind is to see and hear its members. School leadership is an incredibly demanding job. It moves so fast it's likely that you can't remember the last time you took a deep, long breath or checked in with yourself to notice what you are feeling.

Self-awareness is key for effective school leadership. By understanding who you are, what makes you tick, and what ticks you off, a leader can successfully navigate the challenges and emotions of each day. If you don't, there is a cost. "When you don't take the time out to notice and understand your emotions, they have a strange way of resurfacing when you least expect or want them to" (Bradberry & Greaves, 2009, p. 62).

Within the context of a mastermind, a great question to ask members is, "How are you feeling right now?" Allow for plenty of time and space for members to think deeply about their answers. Again, silence is okay.

---

[29] For an opening activities checklist, please see the Resources section in the back matter.

Sometimes I like to ask this question at the beginning of a mastermind, noting how everyone is feeling. Then, at the closing of a mastermind, I'll ask again and show how they've changed. I've never led a meeting where members enter feeling down and leave in a similarly dismal place. That's great for me to see because the process works, but it is even more important for members to note so that they are reminded of the value of the mastermind.

I've noted for a long time that when things get tough in life and leadership, some members' initial response is to run away from the mastermind. I understand the response. It's natural. Even when I am stressed out, I'll look for things to cut to get relief. The problem occurs when members spend more time self-medicating through alcohol, binging Netflix, mindlessly scrolling through social media feeds, and other numbing activities. When leaders are stressed they need to protect their sleep, healthy eating, physical fitness, and support groups.

So, how are you feeling right now?

Reflection questions. These kinds of questions ask participants to dig deep immediately:

- Thinking back to our brief discussion last week on self-care, how have you invested in sustainability this past week?

- What did you learn today?

- Where did you harm a relationship this week, and how will you make amends?

- Tell us about a great decision you made that ended with a poor outcome, or a poor decision you made that ended in a positive outcome.

- What is one idea you will apply from this week's reading to your life and leadership?

Draw a peer. Pair off participants and ask them to draw their colleague for two minutes without looking down at the paper. After the two minutes are up, participants take turns revealing their masterpiece! Before sharing, tell the other person what you hoped to capture and what you appreciate about them. Then share the picture and share a laugh!

What do you have in common? What do you have in common with someone? Name it and then pick who goes next. The goal is to establish a feeling of unity and connection. Google does something similar.[30]

"Imaginary gift" activity. Pair off participants in the mastermind. First, one member hands an imaginary gift to the other member. The receiver names the gift, "Thank you! You got me a [gift name]." The gift giver responds, "I'm so glad you're excited about [gift name]. I got it for you because [fill in the blank]." Then, participants switch roles. This activity is about creativity, knowing the other person, and deep listening. Discuss as a group how this activity made everyone feel and how it relates to school leadership.

"Name it" activity. Slow down your thinking and dip into your imagination. This activity takes place in three rounds. In all rounds participants do the activity concurrently. In Round 1, ask participants to point at objects and name what they see for fifteen seconds (e.g., someone points to a pencil and says "pencil" out loud). In Round 2, participants will have thirty seconds to point at objects, but then name them as if they were

---

[30] They call it "Just like me." Paul Santagata, Head of Industry at Google, created this exercise. Participants name something they share with a coworker and then a Googler adds the phrase "Just like me" to the end of their statement (e.g., "Ariel wants to be fully understood when she shares an idea here, 'just like me.'"). Activities like this are great ways to build emotional intelligence and empathy (Delizonna, 2017).

something else (e.g., someone points to a pencil and says "elephant"). In Round 3, participants do the same as Round 2, but add this directive, "Don't look for patterns or stockpile answers. Go with the flow." This direction is important because in Round 2, participants often alleviate the tension caused by this activity. After the conclusion of Round 3, have a brief discussion about what participants noticed. What was hard? What was easy? How does it apply to leadership, risk-taking, and education?

Nicknames. Once I asked if members had a nickname they go by and what the story was behind the nickname. This was one of my favorite discussions to engage in. The Guiding Principals mastermind cohort really loved this question and to this day refer to each other by their nicknames.[31] We shared so many laughs during this exchange and really got to know each other.

When you were ten years old. Chris Carlson, in the Guiding Principals cohort of the mastermind, created this activity. She wanted to know what our hobbies were when we were ten years old. A mastermind cohort is somewhat large—up to fifteen participants—so for this activity we separated into smaller groups of two or three and rotated leaders through two different groups before coming back together as a large group. A few members were asked to share what they heard[32] and then the entire group was asked where these hobbies and interests show up in our adult life. Asking engaging and personal questions like this within a group increases the interest among mastermind members and produces a psychologically safe environment.

---

[31] Those nicknames included C-L Smooth, Scooter, Chriser, Spike, D-Money, The Professor, Hard Rock, Puck, Smerica, Big Al, The Velvet Hammer, B-Easy, Princess, and (of course) Big Sexy.

[32] By sharing what you enjoyed hearing or learned from other leaders, we intentionally build respect and rapport among the group, which further creates psychological safety in the mastermind.

Permission slips. I learned the idea of "permission slips" from Brené Brown in her book *Dare to Lead.* She describes permission slips as a beginning-of-the-meeting ritual, where participants write down one thing they give themselves permission to do or feel during a meeting (Brown, 2018, p. 53).

So I took Brown's idea and ran with it, embedding it into the mastermind here and there. This activity is brilliant because it helps create a safe space and one that is incredibly intentional. One reason leaders drive mediocre results or show up in a way that is incongruent with their values is because they rush. How can you be your best when you run from meeting to meeting to activity without pausing long enough to consider, with intention, how you want to be in the next moment?

Permission slips slow down our thinking, connect us, and even grow our empathy for others.

In one mastermind, I captured the permission slips that members shared:

> Daniel: "I give myself permission to really listen with both my ears and my eyes in this virtual setting."
>
> Erinn: "Permission to feel tired and run-down but still engaged."
>
> Loren: "I give myself permission to gain a second wind after a tough day."
>
> Jessica: "Permission to listen without feeling the need to fix right away."
>
> Erik: "To be excited, embrace the differences."
>
> Suzanne: "To be optimistic in spite of the horrific news stories."

Beth: "I give myself permission to listen to feedback with an open heart."

Joe: "I give myself permission to turn off the day and focus on just this class!"

What do you give yourself permission to do or feel, right now?

Wins-of-the-week. Often we open by sharing wins-of-the-week within our group. We do this because leaders move from one goal to the next without slowing down and appreciating how far they've come. Leaders are also exposed to a constant barrage of complaints, worries, and other challenges that exist within the community, so focusing on what is working is a powerful reframe and gift to leaders. Wins-of-the-week also help leaders share stories of success when implementing ideas they learned in the mastermind within their community. This activity not only has benefits in terms of self-reflection, hearing the wins of everyone in the mastermind both inspires and challenges members to continue to deliver excellence within their school communities.

Specific Structures

Silence. Silence is powerful. Don't be afraid of it. I am always surprised that leaders have trouble holding silence. We tell our teachers about the importance of "wait time" and challenge teachers to avoid doing the "heavy lifting" (thinking) for students by filling silence with their thoughts or answers to the questions they ask. Some leaders really struggle with silence and fill all the gaps within a group. This kills creativity and robs people of the ability to form and communicate their thoughts. It also hinders your ability to create psychological safety within a group.

Why gather a group together if you are going to answer all the questions as a facilitator? If that's the case, record a video or give a speech. Don't waste other people's time!

Silence is a good thing. The majority of the time silence means you asked a powerful question that is deserving of a well-thought-out answer. If you feel like you need to say something, do this instead—smile and stay quiet.

If you feel uncomfortable in silence, some of your members might feel that way too. Continue to tell everyone that silence is a good thing. Be mindful of those members who seem to dominate discussions and allow little space (if any at all) to other members to share their points of view.

The beauty of silence is that it welcomes deep thinking and invites others to share their perspective.

In a virtual setting, consider coaching mastermind members to stay on mute. This way there is a more democratic way of engaging in discussion. You can't just talk. First, you need to have something worthy to say and then take yourself off mute before engaging.

Silence is a great tool. It builds tension, asks leaders to dig deep and think, and produces psychological safety.

In Chapter 4, I'll introduce two other activities: chat waterfalls and brainwriting. They could easily be shared here in terms of welcoming and increasing psychological safety, but they also fit in nicely with the idea of inclusive environments later in the text.

Agreements. In Chapter 4, we will look at the nine mastermind agreements leaders make and promise to adhere to when participating in our community. One of those agreements is, "Assume positive intent." Not only will you be a lot happier and less stressed, but also by *choosing* to believe that people are doing the best they can, you also build psychological safety within a group. On a larger scale, this is like the idea of pronoia[33], which is the opposite of paranoia. Instead of worrying that the world is out to get you, pronoia is a different stance—that the universe is conspiring *for* you. It's really two sides of the same coin. By choosing curiosity, positive intent, and pronoia, leaders can have a more expansive mindset and create psychological safety within their organizations. Beliefs are not the only way to build psychological safety; you can intentionally do that by encouraging the right behavior as well.

The one big thing. Often, our members are challenged to identify their priority for the coming week. For accountability, members share this priority either verbally or by writing it down so members can follow up with colleagues from week to week. By keeping The One Big Thing tightly focused on a singular goal, leaders leave a mastermind challenged and focused.

Small groups. Since my days in the classroom, I've understood the value of small groups in incorporating all voices. In a smaller group, there is less space to hide and introverts also feel more comfortable sharing thoughts with a handful of peers rather than a whole group. In a virtual setting, we utilize breakout rooms consistently that magically whisk participants to virtual small-group rooms and then return them to a large group at the end of a timer. Rarely are groups formed without a specific prompt or challenge in mind. Usually, leaders are sent to groups with a specific activity or prompt to discuss.

---

[33] My friend Maureen O'Shaughnessy taught this to me during a coaching session. If you are interested in the idea of micro-schools, I highly encourage you to check out Maureen's work at the Micro-School Coalition.

The hot seat. In Chapter 5, we will dig into this topic of the hot seat. For now, it makes sense to briefly describe what the hot seat is and why it builds psychological safety. Each week, one or two members present a challenge, a problem of practice, or a major project they want to complete in the near future. After briefly sharing the context of the issue at hand, the rest of the mastermind then kicks into gear. They might ask clarifying questions, share stories of success and failure, or provide other essential feedback that will help the leader see the issue from a multitude of perspectives. These data are shared by leaders who occupy a similar role, but from around the world. Imagine bringing your number one problem to a group of peers from California to New York; Vancouver to Toronto; and as far south as Argentina and as far east as Malaysia. The quality of feedback would be tremendous, but the secondary benefit of receiving this feedback is that it builds psychological safety.

Engaging All Voices

Rotating facilitators. Out of necessity, I stumbled upon this innovation in the mastermind. For the first year-and-a-half, I facilitated every single mastermind meeting. It wasn't until I became quite sick and needed to miss a mastermind that I asked someone to step in and lead the mastermind as the facilitator. To my relief, everyone showed up the next week, and even better, there was excitement around the idea of permanently rotating mastermind facilitation. This proved to be a worthwhile innovation because it removed me as the "central voice" of the mastermind and invited the unique voices, experiences, and worldviews of all our members to facilitation. Now, each mastermind meeting is open to a world of possibility and members are treated to the specific strengths of individual members. Of everything we do, this one tiny change yielded a big result in terms of benefits.

Brainwriting. This activity will be discussed in more detail in Chapter 4 when we look at building inclusive environments that promote belonging. For the purposes of creating psychological safety, brainwriting asks leaders to write on a given topic prior to the meeting. This helps avoid a confident speaker sharing first and setting the tone for the discussion. Since everyone writes their ideas prior to the meeting, you are much more likely to hear diverse ideas during the discussion. The other benefit is that it provides time for introverts to process their thoughts on their own time prior to engaging with the entire mastermind. Facilitators can also encourage members to present other colleagues' ideas via their brainwriting, which helps build respect for other points of view.

Donut pals. Members are encouraged to connect outside of the formal meeting time each week. We call this meeting "donut pals" because members are encouraged to connect over coffee, tea, and maybe a donut. This happens within and between different cohorts and adds value to individual members because it expands their professional learning network. Individuals connect over education and leadership, but they are also encouraged to talk about life, dreams, hopes, and goals as well. As a result of this, members have made plans for mastermind meetups, and because of identifying shared goals and interests, a number of professional partnerships have been formed as well.

Now that we have an understanding of how the mastermind creates psychological safety, let's turn our focus to how it promotes self-awareness.

Mastermind Case Study
Colin Hogan
Head of School at Learning Community Charter School

"Things are better today, because of you."

Tell us what you do and what your work typically entails.

I serve as the principal and chief school administrator of the most diverse school in New Jersey. I oversee curriculum, staff development, and facilities; collaborate with our board of trustees; and, most importantly, do everything possible to make school a place that empowers our students, faculty, and families to make a difference in their communities.

How has the mastermind helped you?

Learning Community Charter School is its own school district, so having a network of school administrators to learn from, lean on, and support means everything to me. I've learned how to be a better leader and a better person from the incredible leaders I've met in the mastermind.

What's the best part of the mastermind?

The community we've established. I've been in this group since the very beginning, and I've met many incredible leaders from my mastermind and in other Better Leaders Better Schools cohorts. We've met through video chat and in person. What I always find amazing about everyone in the group is that they are driven by a purpose and mission to serve their kids, schools, and communities. When I am having a difficult time as a leader, I always leave masterminds feeling recharged and ready to face challenges ahead in the coming week.

What is one way the mastermind has helped you approach leadership differently?

I think as a leader there are certain styles and approaches that we all gravitate toward. The diversity of members in the mastermind has made me consider new perspectives and new strategies. This makes me better at serving my own diverse school community. Ultimately, I'm going to do something that resonates and works for someone else and that is due to the vast experience of the mastermind members.

What advice would you give a leader considering joining the mastermind?

If you are ready to be brave, bold, and vulnerable, this is the right place for you. You will be challenged but also lifted up. Be ready to think, laugh, and grow. If your goal is to add to your leadership family, there is nowhere better than the mastermind.

Anything else you'd like to say about the mastermind?

I think the kindness and empathy that define this group matters so much. We care about each other and just understand how much we need each other as we travel through school leadership. Sometimes a member as far away as Australia will call me just to check in and that just makes such a difference.

Self-awareness

Just beyond

yourself.

It's where

you need

to be.

Half a step

into

self-forgetting

and the rest

restored

by what

you'll meet.

–David Whyte, "Just Beyond Yourself"

I opened this section of Chapter 3 with an excerpt from David Whyte's "Just Beyond Yourself." The poem illustrates a challenge that every leader faces—the barriers constructed by our own two hands. The idea that the answer lies "just beyond yourself" resonates with me. Too often I am reminded of how I get in my own way. I dislike conflict. I have the ability to successfully navigate tough conversations, but this does not come easily to me. My default is to ignore what needs to be corrected and avoid conversations that surface conflict. In Texas, I inherited three assistant principals (APs) when I was hired. About halfway through the year, I found out that the most seasoned AP on my staff had applied for my position as principal, but failed to even get an interview. With hindsight, I now understand why she seemed to dislike me and, worse, actively worked to undermine my authority. By the time I had learned all this, I had already resigned from my position and decided on pursuing Better Leaders Better Schools full time. I avoided every hard conversation I needed to have with her. This poisoned our culture and limited the effectiveness of the school under my leadership. To this day, I count that as one of my biggest leadership failures. Instead of being overcome by shame, I decided to use this failure as a learning experience and opportunity to explore why I gave this toxic teammate so much power. Too bad I didn't have Whyte's poem at the time. The idea of "self-forgetting" I read as the grace we give ourselves and the power of not holding on to grudges or replaying our mistakes over and over.

Whyte also comments how we are "restored" by what we'll meet just beyond ourselves. I interpret this as the gift of courageous exploration and development of self-awareness. My leadership failure stemmed from a grave ignorance of what was going on inside of me, and then, how to reconcile those emotions with the negative behavior I experienced at the hands of my AP.

According to the Center for Creative Leadership (CCL), "Leadership success starts with authenticity—doing our jobs without compromising our values and personality." And it leads to organizations that "have engaged, enthusiastic, motivated employees and psychologically safe cultures." In the CCL article "Authentic Leadership: What It Is, Why It Matters" (2020), the post posits five ways leaders can be more authentic:

1. Rethink "leadership image."

2. Increase your self-awareness.

3. Assess your values, likes, and dislikes.

4. Take action, but get support.

5. Work on effective communication.

For the remainder of this section, we will focus on the idea of increasing our self-awareness.

Two-Thirds of Us Have No Clue . . .

Over the years, TalentSmart has tested 500,000+ leaders regarding emotional intelligence (EQ), and they found that only 36 percent of the leaders tested could accurately identify their emotions as they happen. This shocking statistic means that two-thirds of leaders have no idea what is going on inside themselves, and as a result, their emotions control their thoughts and actions (Bradberry & Greaves, 2009, p. 13).

Self-awareness was certainly not taught to me as a secondary or postsecondary student. Emotional intelligence was not a part of the assessment that resulted in my principal licensure. We are primarily emotional beings. The psychologist Jonathan Haidt is known for saying, "The emotional tail wags the rational dog" (as cited in Kahneman, 2011, p. 140). The reason for that is quite simple. As we collect data via our senses, that information enters our brains from our spinal cord and must pass through our limbic system, where we feel, before entering the front of the brain, where we think rationally (Bradberry & Greaves, 2009, pp. 6–7).

What is the cost of two-thirds of school leaders being controlled by their emotions? As I shared in the previous section, the cost for me was that I avoided crucial conversations I needed to have with my colleague. Left alone, our culture ultimately suffered for it and it created dysfunction within our administrative team and influenced certain faculty negatively. This could have been avoided if I was more aware of what was going on internally.

Although emotional intelligence is not taught in school, we do teach it in the mastermind. TalentSmart also found that "83 percent of people high in self-awareness are top performers, and just two percent of bottom performers are high in self-awareness" (Bradberry & Greaves, 2009, p. 26). Self-aware leaders are authentic leaders. They are also effective. Professional development that encourages, teaches, and nurtures self-awareness creates better leaders.[34]

> Self-aware leaders are authentic leaders. They are also effective.

---

[34] It also pays to be a self-aware leader. Bradberry and Greaves's (2009) research shows a direct link between EQ and earning potential. Based on their emotional intelligence survey, every point increase of EQ adds an additional $1300 in annual salary (p. 21). Cha-ching!

Perfect or Good Enough?

A lack of self-awareness does more than just limit your effectiveness as a leader; it can also kill you. I coach many high performers who are at times crippled by their desire to be the best, improve their skills, and attain the impossible—a perfect performance. Type-A driven leaders have been able to climb the ladder of success quickly by creating results through hard work and sheer determination. But this isn't a sustainable practice nor the most effective. It can have disastrous results on a leader's health.

Working at an unsustainable pace comes with a very real cost. Eblin (2017) notes that giving too much professionally and neglecting your self-care results in negative health outcomes leading to higher rates of heart disease, anxiety, ulcers, cancer, and premature aging. In a study of principals in Australia, Riley (2016) found that school leaders scored below the general population in terms of well-being. All positive measures (e.g., self-worth) were lower and negative measures (e.g., stress) were higher (as cited in O'Neill & Glasson, 2018, p. 889).

A lack of self-awareness prevents leaders from checking in with themselves and being able to see how their work cadence is negatively impacting their lives. By the time they realize the real damage they are causing to their health, it may be too late.[35]

A mastermind can help a leader focus on their well-being and create a better sense of work–life harmony. Each new member immediately plugs into a powerful network. The diversity of experience and worldviews

---

[35] It was too late for Trish Antulov, who was found dead at her desk by her husband. Her husband said this about Mrs. Antulov's work life, "She just didn't have time to look after herself properly. She was under a lot of stress and terrible pressure just to be successful in her job." Trish Antulov was 65 years old (Reid, as cited in Hiatt, 2018).

helps new members see there is a different way, and their tightly held definitions of leadership are able to evolve within the protective boundaries of our community. In the mind of an overachiever, perfect is the goal and anything less is failure.[36]

Many leaders also approach all tasks as equal. The board report, the teacher debrief, and the weekly newsletter all need to get done. They don't require nor get the same amount of energy and time invested, but leaders often use the same kind of focus and quality control as if the tasks are equal. The tasks are not equal, and here is a secret about top performers: they know that not everything you do has to be "A"-level effort. Some things can be turned in as a "C"- or even a "D"-level effort. Done is often better than perfect.

After hearing that perspective, many administrators are seeing the world in a new light for the first time. This perspective forces a leader to have clear priorities and block time out for those tasks equal to the importance of the task. A simple shift in seeing can unleash incredible results within a leader's organization. By identifying the significant tasks in the day and limiting the amount of time spent on insignificant tasks two things happen: the leader finds more time to invest into the work that really matters and produces value for the school, and the leader finds more time to spend on themselves and with their family. With one shift of perspective, the quality of both work and life improves.

I call this addition by subtraction.

Doing great work is not synonymous with perfection. It makes no sense to obsess over every detail if it is killing you. School will take and take and take from you if you allow it to. When you are on your deathbed, do you

---

[36] I should know. I am a recovering perfectionist. How depressing!

think you'll feel great that you responded to every email and created every school improvement plan perfectly?

Fostering a sense of self-awareness helps leaders become cognizant of the emotional landscape within. With that kind of understanding, they can be more real, and when leaders are authentic, anything is possible. The emotional terrain is important to note with self-awareness and so are the stories we tell ourselves.

Between the Frames

I developed my love for reading at Fat Dutchie's Comic Book Shoppe in Palatine, Illinois. The owner, Chuck, played a pivotal role in my young life. In middle school, I would ride my bike every day to Fat Dutchie's and endlessly window shop for baseball cards, action figurines, and comics. Since I was always there, Chuck must have figured, "I might as well hire the kid."

I would count the inventory of comics for Chuck so he would know how many books to order in future months and estimate sales. I was paid weekly in lunch, Chicago-style pizza or Italian beef; twenty dollars; and in comic books. My favorite superhero was Spider-Man; I related to the nerd who was awkward around peers (and especially girls) but had tremendous potential.

To this day, I still love comics. I recently read Scott McCloud's graphic novel, *Understanding Comics*. This is a wonderful history of comics and the structure of great storytelling. Scott also highlighted one of the reasons the comic is such an innovative art form and a favorite of mine: the magic happens in between frames.

The comic is an interesting art form in that it leaves a lot of information off the page. Antoine de Saint-Exupéry said it best: "Perfection is achieved, not when there is nothing more to add, but when there is nothing left to take away." This is what comics do. Between the first frame and the second, it is up to the reader to fill in the blanks. We all tell ourselves stories. They are based on our assumptions and informed by our experiences. Self-awareness helps us see the inner narrative that is constantly going on.[37] In Chapter 2, I talked about how our beliefs inform our actions. When our beliefs are built on solid ground, this is fine, but too often our beliefs are built on something we heard (and didn't verify) or on faulty assumptions.

Through consistent dialogue with other school professionals, the mastermind helps leaders see the amount of power and choice they have regarding the inner narratives that influence our behavior. If you are experiencing negative outcomes at work, one area you should check is the inner dialogue you are having at work. Sometimes getting a better outcome is as easy as telling ourselves a better story. Connecting with a group of like-minded peers allows the space for leaders to develop self-awareness. They do this by investigating the narratives they tell themselves and exploring them in a psychologically safe space where counternarratives—often more accurate— are able to be shared and internalized. With each revision of the stories we tell ourselves, our self-awareness and authenticity grow. So does our impact.

Wins-of-the-Week

In the previous section, I shared how the wins-of-the-week activity helps build psychological safety. It also

---

[37] Here, I'd like to share that of all the techniques I've attempted myself, a mindfulness practice will help you grow exponentially. Mindfulness has taught me to note what is going on inside me, including the stories and emotions I experience. Equally important is to note without judging and to notice how quickly the emotion or story dissipates before a new one appears. If there is one practice that will help grow your self-awareness, this is it.

helps build self-awareness. Many leaders I work with struggle with celebrating wins. For some, it's because they are moving too fast—from observation, to parent meeting, to department meeting, and so on. Other leaders are constantly in motion in relation to goals. They achieve goal "x" and before unpacking what made them successful and what could be improved, and celebrating the accomplishment, they begin sprinting toward the next goal.

We start nearly every mastermind with wins-of-the-week. Members are encouraged to reflect on the past week and briefly (ninety seconds or less) share what they consider a "win." Wins can be personal or professional. The point of the exercise is to slow down and celebrate the progress members of our community have accomplished.

Leadership is much more enjoyable when we find time to relish our accomplishments. In my view, leadership should be fun. If it isn't, why dedicate our lives to this labor? The wins-of-the-week activity is not to pat our own back or to increase our ego. School leaders are the epitome of servant-leaders. Educators serve. They look to the needs of others before their own. We have huge hearts. But there is a cost to this kind of selfless leadership. This activity challenges us to relish our achievements. There is great value in celebration.

As a leader of leaders, I push those I serve to pause and think about what they've accomplished both big and small. In the context of the mastermind, we spend five minutes at the start of most meetings sharing what we've done and accomplished. When working on larger goals, not only will we backward map how to get there, we also plan the celebration both as a team and as an individual. This is an important part of the process. Team celebrations are easy; individual ones much harder. After accomplishing a major goal, maybe you get a massage or pedicure. Maybe it's a vacation. I find that it's fun to plan that out in the goal-setting process and celebrate the wins-of-the-week along the way.

Respond to the Data

In the mastermind, leaders often are invited to complete a check-in survey. This was birthed out of the coronavirus pandemic as I saw leaders increasingly stressed and I grew worried about their physical and emotional health. It's impossible to check in with each member each week. The survey allowed me to prioritize who to reach out to. There are a number of questions, but only the first two are mandatory: the member's name and a Likert-style survey that goes from "I am in crisis" to "Everything is great."

The next nine questions are optional and act as a mirror for the leader. They are simple yes/no questions to remind a leader what will help them through this difficult time. These questions were designed to build self-awareness since they force the leader to consider what's going on inside them and if they are prioritizing their health.

The questions are as follows:

- Are you intentionally planning "buffer time," "white space," or time for mindfulness to recenter each day?

- Are you intentionally planning "turn off time" (limiting screen time, news, email)?

- Are you intentionally planning physical time (stretching, walking, working out, etc.)?

- Are you intentionally planning time in nature?

- Are you intentionally planning balance time (time dedicated just for you or with friends/family)?

- Are you getting enough sleep?

- Are you eating a healthy diet?

- Are you saying "No" and honoring your needed boundaries?

- Are you practicing gratitude?

If leaders are answering mostly "yes" to these questions, I am more confident that they are doing well. If the answers to those questions are a string of "nos," then I know a crisis is looming. The reflective nature of the questions is enough for some leaders to take stock of where they are and what needs to change. If they feel like it's out of their control or they require additional help, then the next two questions present an opportunity to ask for help.

The last two questions are open-ended and also optional. This tells me potentially how I can help or if I can connect the leader to a resource that might help. The open-ended questions are as follows:

- Do you have a problem?

- What do you need?

Psychologically safe spaces help leaders experience authenticity. So does a high degree of self-awareness. The final piece of the authenticity puzzle is being values-driven. When there is alignment between our thoughts, feelings, and actions, our leadership is authentic and effective. Being values-driven is a key component to this alignment and what we will explore next.

Mastermind Case Study
Karine Veldhoen
Chief Learning Officer at Willowstone Academy

"The future belongs to the story-tellers and the connectors."
–Leonard Sweet

Tell us what you do and what your work typically entails.

Typically I am strategically leading three organizations: an independent school in British Columbia called Willowstone Academy, an educational consultancy platform called Learn Forward, and a charity doing education projects in East Africa called Niteo.

How has the mastermind helped you?

First of all, the mastermind introduced me to school leaders from around the world who challenge and sharpen my leadership. I found my complex vocational landscape a lonely place. So, the camaraderie I found in the mastermind is holy water for me.

Second, I am grateful for the gifts of like-minded change-makers who always bring fresh ideas, hard-earned wisdom, and encouragement to share at each meeting. I always leave with a situation reframed in my own mind, a leadership strategy to apply, or a reminder with a big cloud around it in my journal.

Finally, the mastermind invites me into interesting work. I become a more capable leader through the research-based readings and the accountability to intentionally apply them. Each meeting is a place of inspiration to grow and learn. And, as far as I am concerned, there was never a more important time to be a capable and high-caliber educational leader for the sake of the children.

What's the best part of the mastermind?

Laughing along the way is the best part for me. I take myself **way** too seriously, and my mastermind friends help me remember to enjoy the journey. It is a gift to me.

What is one way the mastermind has helped you approach leadership differently?

I am consistently reminded to make time for reflection, big-picture thinking, and margin. Danny gives every leader the permission we need to hear to "work smarter, not harder." The consistency is something I really need in my life to make this practice a reality.

What advice would you give a leader considering joining the mastermind?

If you think you might need it, you needed it six months ago. It's the perfect place to be nourished and also "level up" in your professional life.

Anything else you'd like to say about the mastermind?

I can't wait to see you there!

Values-Driven

"He who has a why to live for can bear almost any how."

–Viktor Frankl

Let Your Values Guide You

Viktor Frankl was a Jew who survived the Holocaust. His experience in the concentration camps informed his work as a psychologist and as an author years later.[38] Frankl has taught me the power of choice we all have, even in a horrific environment like Auschwitz. Life in the concentration camps taught Frankl that we either let life happen to us and accept it as fate, or we choose how to navigate life despite the circumstances we face.

---

[38] Frankl's book *Man's Search for Meaning* is cited by many leaders as influential in their thinking. I consider this work as one of the best I've read and it holds a spot in my book "hall of fame."

We who lived in concentration camps can remember the men who walked through the huts comforting others, giving away their last piece of bread. They may have been few in number, but they offer sufficient proof that everything can be taken from a man but one thing: the last of the human freedoms— to choose one's attitude in any given set of circumstances, to choose one's own way.

And there were always choices to make. Every day, every hour . . . (Frankl, 2006, pp. 65–66)

Frankl created the theory of logotherapy, which essentially means you accept the responsibility of being the author of your own life and living in accordance with your values. In fact, Frankl said it this way, "Man is pushed by drives, but is pulled by values" (Frankl, as cited in Holiday, 2016, p. 99).

This quote and the one that opened this section both identify the importance of being values-driven. But do leaders truly understand what their core values are? What are the principles that guide their lives? What values are they so committed to, they are willing to be punished for them?

In my experience coaching school administrators, leaders have a general sense of values, but they aren't available to be recalled at a moment's notice and they certainly don't consistently inform the choices these leaders make on a daily basis.

Just like rushing from one goal to the next, life and leadership can *feel* like a blizzard of never-ending tasks, requests on our time, and emergencies. If leaders aren't careful, this experience may feel like they are the ball in a pinball machine, constantly ricocheting off obstacles and being slapped around the game without any control over the direction of their lives.

There is a difference between shallow work and deep work. The challenge is to separate the two and understand which is most important. It feels good to strike things off our to-do list, but this loses sight of what is most important and most impactful to the organization. Even worse, rarely do the shallow items on our to-do list help leaders live in accordance with their values.

If you've ever done something only to regret it later, you have acted in violation of your values.

One memorable time I violated my values involved a colleague, a book room, and a key.

One Day I Ignored My Values

At the time I was an instructional coach serving in a selective enrollment high school on the far south side of Chicago.[39] My colleague was the worst teacher I've ever seen, and her classroom held the access to the English Department's book room. She was frequently absent from school, and as a result, the rest of the English teachers did not have access to the books they needed for instruction because the door was locked. After watching this cycle a number of times, I decided to take action. Morally, I was right to act. The teachers, and thus the students, did not have the materials they

---

[39] Our school was situated between the Roseland and Pullman neighborhoods. Roseland is the home of the "Wild 100s," where gun fights and other violence often break out on the streets. It is also where Barack Obama got his start as a young politician. The historic Pullman neighborhood was built by George Pullman so that his employees had access to housing that was close to work and included modern amenities such as indoor plumbing, gas, and sewers. Workers initiated the Pullman strike in 1894, which was a major turning point in US labor law. It turns out that decreasing wages while maintaining high rents is not good for business!

needed in order to be successful. The remedy was easy and clear—teachers (and students) should have access to materials when they needed them. Fortunately for the English teachers, I had a key that opened both my colleague's classroom and the book room, and I decided to start opening both rooms when she was absent.

What I failed to realize in the moment was how she would take that personally. Specifically, she was worried that I might steal and leak union materials to the building's administration. I never would do that; my sole purpose was to create access to the books teachers and students needed. But my colleague couldn't possibly know my intentions, and we didn't have the trust needed for her to assume positive intent at the time. As a result, a difficult conversation was needed.

In preparation, I read and reread *Crucial Conversations* by Kerry Patterson, Joseph Grenny, Ron McMillan, and Al Switzler. I took ample notes and scripted out how the difficult conversation might go. I practiced over and over again.

And then real life happened.

My colleague didn't respond according to the script I had prepared. In hindsight, we were arguing over two different things.[40] I was arguing that teachers and students should have access to the book room at any time. She was arguing that confidential union materials were housed in her classroom[41] and when I opened her classroom I violated her domain. As a result, my colleague requested that I turn in my key to the

---

[40] There is an actual name for this common phenomenon. When two different topics are being discussed during a difficult conversation, this is called "switchtracking." I learned this after reading *Thanks for the Feedback* within the mastermind.

[41] Never mind that they were locked in a cabinet and she had the only key.

principal so I didn't have access to her classroom, the book room, and the confidential union materials she was concerned about.

If I was having that conversation today, I hope I would have noticed that our discussion was heading into troubling territory.[42] The best path forward actually would have been to take two steps back and reconvene when our emotions were under control and the temperature of the conversation was lowered. Given time and space, a younger and more immature version of myself might have recognized that we were arguing two different points. This factor would have led to a more productive discussion and maybe even the outcome I desired.

Instead, this is what I did . . .

When my colleague requested that I turn in my key, I held the key just inches from her nose and said, "I'll never, ever turn in this key" and walked out of her room.

In that moment, I was the worse version of myself and violated my values. I did champion the cause of the English teachers and students, but at a terrible cost. I was such a jerk that day!

So what could I have done differently?

The Power of Developing Your Emotional Intelligence

If my values truly informed my choices, I would need to have done the hard work of identifying those values, thinking about how they show up in my work, and recognizing when I am in the midst of violating them. At the time of this major leadership blunder, I had not made the investment in identifying those values precisely.

---

[42] Kenny Loggins might even call it "The Danger Zone."

To avoid leadership violations of your core values, you should ask yourself, "What values do I wish to live by?" Next, you can take a sheet of paper and create two columns. Write in the left column all your core values. In the right column write any recent things you've done or said that violate that core value. The Stoic philosopher Seneca put this into practice in approximately 63 AD. This is timeless advice.

> I shall put myself under observation straight away and undertake a review of my day—a course which is of utmost benefit. What really ruins our characters is the fact that none of us looks back over his life. We think about what we are going to do, and only rarely of that, and fail to think about what we have done, yet any plans for the future are dependent on the past. (Seneca, ca. 63–65/2004, p. 140)

This can be difficult to do because it is painful to admit where we have performed poorly. In isolation, this kind of deep and honest reflection is nearly impossible. Surrounded by a trusted group of peers, this kind of challenging reflection becomes easier. In the mastermind, we'll discuss the following reflection question in a whole-group or small-group setting:

> Where in the last week did you violate one of your core values?

By creating the space to have this courageous conversation, leaders are willing to risk admitting where they have fallen short. This doesn't happen in internal district professional development. It rarely happens in outside professional development focused on student achievement, attendance, discipline, and so on. It takes a special kind of community, one where members are willing to look within and develop our emotional intelligence because we believe it is there, in our inner worlds, that the best leaders are developed.

Whether you are leading in isolation or surrounded by a nurturing community of peers, this kind of reflection doesn't work unless you first have developed your core values. Experience will also teach you that it's easy to live out your values when the job is also running smoothly, but when the stakes get higher, or worse, when you're in the middle of a crisis, this is when the hard work of defining your values and the years spent reflecting and examining your words and actions will bear fruit. This is exactly why I failed in a difficult conversation with my colleague concerning access to the book room in Chicago and why I failed to confront my AP's toxicity in Texas.

Internal Values

> You've wandered all over and finally realized that you never found what you were after: how to live. Not in syllogisms, not in money, or fame, or self-indulgence. Nowhere. Then where is it to be found? In doing what human nature requires. How? Through first principles. Which should govern your intentions and your actions. (Aurelius, ca. 161–180/2003, p. 101)

One of my coaching mentors, Rich Litvin, taught me a coaching mantra that I recite each day in order to prepare myself mentally for serving leaders—"I help powerful people remember how powerful they are." It's an inspiring mantra and helps me remember that those I serve often forget how powerful they are. Recently, I sent a text to a coaching client asking how the journaling on two specific questions I assigned her was going. She responded, "It's going poorly" and then went on to tell me how badly her supervisor was treating her.[43]

As her coach, it was easy to see that she didn't answer the question and that her focus was on her perceived mistreatment at the hands of her supervisor. What this leader forgot is that she is powerful. She has a choice. A useful reframe of her experience could have been how her supervisor was a "gift" that would allow her to practice living out her values.

The Marcus Aurelius quote that starts this section speaks to the power of living by your core values ("first principles," according to Aurelius). As I said earlier as well, living out your core values is easy when things are running smooth. When times are challenging, core values are easily abandoned. And that is part of the "rub." At least for me, when I violate my first principles I begin to beat myself up in my head. I focus on the negative and say terrible things to myself that I would never say to another human being. If I'm not aware of what is happening, this negative cycle becomes darker and darker until I am the worst version of myself. Some call this our "shadow" self.[44]

The irony is that I challenged my client to journal on one of her values that wasn't consistently being demonstrated at work. She received challenging feedback from not only her supervisor, but also her peers—feedback she had never heard in any other work environment.

---

[43] I can relate. In a difficult situation I learned that I had the power to let go of my grievances and move on. It could be as easy as a choice. Marcus Aurelius's thoughts on this matter helped me, and they can help you too if you find yourself in this situation. He said, "Choose not to be harmed—and you won't be harmed. Don't feel harmed—and you haven't been" (Aurelius, ca. 161–180/2003, p. 39).

[44] Jerry Colonna's book *Reboot* explores this topic and how to wrestle with your emotions and ultimately grow up.

As part of the course correction, I asked her to journal on that core value to see what she noticed. Journaling is one of the most powerful tools for self-aware leaders.

Earlier, I mentioned how Seneca would review the day to see where he lived out his values and where he fell short. Marcus Aurelius did this as well. He called his first principles "epithets" and identified them as follows: upright, modest, straightforward, sane, cooperative, disinterested (Aurelius, ca. 161–180/2003, p. 134). These values guided his words and deeds each day. The alignment between epithets and actions allowed him to lead authentically.

I hope you see the value in journaling and identifying the values you wish to live by. Another useful tool I'll introduce to you next is creating a personal philosophy.

When you experience stress and tension so vividly that it's hard to focus, are you able to navigate those murky waters and find stillness and clarity?

Years ago I invested in an online course called "Compete to Create" developed by Dr. Michael Gervais and Coach Pete Carroll. The course is about the mindset of top performers, and I invested in this course to learn how to develop a "personal philosophy." A personal philosophy is a five-to-ten-word phrase that is a leader's compass when navigating each day. Coach Pete Carroll's personal philosophy is "Always compete." Dr. Michael Gervais's personal philosophy is "Every day is an opportunity to create a living masterpiece."

I was sold on the idea that I needed a philosophy that guided my work every day, much like how the Stoics used their epithets. My first draft was done in a day, but it took about a year of drilling down until I nailed it.

My personal philosophy is "Be an intentional catalyst."

In just four words, I was able to capture the essence of everything I want to be. My whole life I have noticed how my presence changes the energy in a room. And like anything in life, there are two sides to this coin. At my worst, I suffocate the creativity, warmth, and connection in a space. At my best, I do the opposite; I see and help others see the opportunity and potential all around them.

In the early 2000s, I was a teacher at Franklin Middle School in Champaign, Illinois. In addition to teaching reading and writing, I also taught AVID and was the site director.[45] Because of the AVID program and the fact that the University of Illinois campus was in our back yard, we exposed our students to college life frequently. After one field trip I coordinated, we brought a hundred kids or so back to our campus in time for a late lunch. We had ordered an obscene amount of Little Caesars pizza.[46] I wasn't there to receive the order. Some colleagues were "kind" enough to send the pizzas to the appropriate classrooms.

But . . . I hadn't communicated my plan of which pizzas went to which classrooms. Usually not a big deal if all the pizzas were generally the same.

This should not have been a big deal *at all*. I blew up. I scolded my colleagues and gave them a dirty look. I was such a jerk.[47]

---

[45] Eventually our school became an AVID distinguished school. By then I had left to teach in Chicago, but I was lucky enough to come back and consult for the school and help them prepare for the site visits that earned them the award they had worked on for years.

[46] As a native Chicagoan, I can say that Little Caesars *is not* actually pizza. It is a "pizza-like" substance with great value at five dollars a pie. Real pizza includes Lou Malnati's, Gino's East, Connie's, or Giordano's. If you haven't eaten at any of these fine establishments, the fact is, you haven't had pizza.

[47] You could also describe me in that moment with a word that rhymes with "masshole."

At the time, I didn't have a personal philosophy or first principles to guide me. I was caught up in my emotions. I was both angry and afraid. Angry that my colleagues took initiative. Fearful that all the pizza would be gobbled up and some kids would be left hungry. Fearful that it would have been my fault and that my colleagues would think less of me.

I was less mature then and didn't realize how my emotions influenced my behavior. These days, because I consistently engage in journaling and practice mindfulness, I can tell when I'm starting to get upset. I feel it in my body—my breathing becomes shallow. I clench my jaw. My fists may even be balled up as if I'm ready to fight. And because I've done the hard work to identify my personal philosophy, I can hear a faint whisper, "Be an intentional catalyst," and in a moment I can correct my course.

When you live by your values, you live in alignment and authentically. When you teach it to others and reflect on your core values or personal philosophy you design your life with great intention and hold yourself accountable to living in alignment with your personal philosophy.

A personal philosophy or identification of core values is important, and as a leader you should do the hard work to develop these on your own. Organizations also have values, which can be used as a starting point for discussion and reflection around the alignment of values and actions. If you'd like to create your own personal philosophy you have two options:

1. Invest in the "Compete to Create" program developed by Dr. Michael Gervais and Coach Pete Carroll.

2. Visit the Better Leaders Better Schools website and join our mailing list. We offer

workshops throughout the year, one being on how to create your own personal philosophy. Invites go out to our email subscribers.

Group Values

Prior to joining their first meeting, a new member is sent an onboarding document with a variety of items on it, one being a description of each of our core values. Since the first component of powerful professional development is authenticity, one way mastermind members experience this is by having short discussions on one core value during a meeting. Questions we may consider include the following:

- How have you lived out this value today?

- Where did you miss the mark living out this core value in the past week?

- Where did you see this value demonstrated in the mastermind?

- Where did you see this value lived out in your school community?

- What is easy about this core value?

- What is hard about this core value?

As you can see, the questions are simple on the surface and have more depth the longer we reflect and the further we go in our mastermind discussions. Conversations like these encourage our members to reflect on what they say and do in a given day and if they are aligned with our values. Like Seneca, nearly 2000 years earlier, we ask our members to review their day and be the best version of leader they can be.

What follows is a brief description of our mastermind core values.

Lead like Madiba

One of my heroes is Nelson Mandela (known as "Madiba" in Xhosa, his mother tongue). When I think of a leader, he is one of the first people who enters my mind. He spent twenty-seven years in prison, where his oppressors worked to break his spirit through poor living conditions and back-breaking work.

When Madiba was freed from prison, he became the first black president of South Africa and was known for his preference for reconciliation versus revenge.

Madiba embodied many great leadership principles, but one that I think he emulated better than most is that leadership is a generous act of service. To Madiba, leadership is a humane endeavor.

He cared more about reconciliation than revenge. He didn't care about winning as an individual, but winning as a whole. Madiba also was playing an infinite game (the one we are playing as leaders). For us to win, you don't have to lose.

That's what it means to me to lead like Madiba.

Take the leap

If we're not here to grow, what's the point?

In the mastermind, we are about taking action even when it's not necessarily comfortable.

(Continued)

(Continued)

I think leadership can be scary. Years ago I rode a water roller coaster with my nephews Silas and Levi. At the time, Levi was young and just tall enough to get on the ride. Silas was cool as a cucumber the entire time, but Levi was a nervous wreck. When we first got on the ride, Levi was fine, but once he realized that we'd have to come back down from the height we had been slowly climbing . . . that's when he lost it!

He wanted out!

But that wasn't a choice.

We made it to the edge, right before our boat was to dive. Levi was screaming with fear.

And then we dropped . . .

And we screamed for the next ten seconds.

We made it to the bottom safely, and within seconds the screams turned to laughter.

Levi kept giggling, "I can't stop laughing. I can't stop laughing. Can we do it again?"

Leadership is also a lot like a roller coaster. You take the leap. You dance with fear. You take action. And you do it again.

Whole hearts and whole selves

I wanted to call this value "Bring your best self," but after reading Brené Brown's *Dare to Lead*, I changed it based on her definition of

> Leadership is also a lot like a roller coaster. You take the leap. You dance with fear. You take action. And you do it again.

wholeheartedness: engaging in our lives from a place of worthiness. It means cultivating the courage, compassion, and connection to wake up in the morning and think, no matter what gets done and how much is left undone, I am enough.

The idea of enough means that we are complete. We are enough. And it starts with us. If you are waiting for me, other mastermind members, your staff, your spouse, your friends, or your family to validate you, you could be waiting a long time.

It's also unfair. Don't put that burden on other people to make you feel good about yourself.

Start from a place of worth. Bring your best self each week to the mastermind by leading with whole hearts and whole selves.

If we do that as leaders, we absolutely will bring our best selves to the mastermind. Stay curious. Be compassionate (to yourself).

Rule #6

Rule #6 is also inspired by *The Art of Possibility* (Zander & Zander, 2002, p. 79). In that text the authors describe the meaning behind this rule via a story using two political dignitaries as the protagonists. I have adapted the story to include school leaders to illustrate the point of Rule #6 below.

(Continued)

(Continued)

A school principal and her newly hired AP are in a conference room discussing the mission and vision of the school during a new hire onboarding day.

Suddenly a woman bursts in, the ninth-grade counselor. She is clearly upset and begins to shout, jump up and down, and bang her fists on the cedar conference table.

"This is an emergency!" she exclaims.

The principal looks at the counselor, "Michelle, don't forget Rule #6."

Instantly Michelle regroups and collects herself, apologizes to the two administrators, and leaves a changed human being.

The new AP notes this sudden change but doesn't mention anything, and the two administrators get back to their onboarding discussion.

Thirty minutes later the principal and AP are again interrupted. This time the custodian barges in slamming the door open, jumping up and down, and beating on the cedar conference table.

"The damn pipes . . . they've burst! Water is everywhere. We're going to drown!"

Seeing the custodian was quite dry, the principal calmly responds, "James, don't forget Rule #6."

Calm washes over the custodian, who collects himself, regroups, apologizes to the administrators, and thanks the principal for her wise advice.

The AP notes the sudden change of character, but doesn't mention anything after the custodian leaves.

The onboarding discussion continues, but after another thirty minutes the AP interrupts the principal.

"Excuse me, Amy. I've never seen anything quite like this culture. We have been talking about mission, vision, and values this entire day, but we haven't addressed any of the rules, specifically Rule #6. Do you mind sharing what Rule #6 means?"

"Of course," replies the principal. "Don't take yourself so damn seriously."

"Okay," says the AP. "That is one heck of a rule."

After thinking some more the AP then asks, "Do you mind telling me what the other rules are here?"

"Of course," replies the principal. "There are no other rules."

At the end of the day, Rule #6 is the most important rule. The work of school leadership is serious and should be treated as such, but that

(Continued)

(Continued)

doesn't mean we need to take ourselves too seriously. Nobody likes to be around a leader who is wound too tight.

Keep making a ruckus!

At the center of what we do as leaders is this: we make change happen.

I love the word *ruckus*.

Mastermind members are the epitome of ruckus makers: those out-of-the-box leaders making change happen in education.

We improve every context in which we lead because we always leave it better than we found it.

In dysfunctional and failing schools, it's easy to see what needs to be fixed. And we fix it.

But even in healthy, high-performing organizations, there is an opportunity to grow as well.

In fact, leading in this kind of environment might even be more challenging because the status quo is safe. It's comfortable. The need to change is less apparent and not talked about.

A ruckus maker helps others see. With a new perspective we see

- Potential

- Possibility

- Opportunity

- Abundance

Ruckus makers know that they are playing an infinite game. There are no clear start and finish lines. No clear winners and losers. We all can actually win, playing the same game.

This is different from a seventh-place trophy. We don't give those out.

What this means is that we expect excellence and that you don't have to lose for me to win.

This kind of perspective fuels our tank as we embark on the journey causing a ruckus and making change in education.

The Edges

One of my mentors is Seth Godin. Years ago, I learned the importance of positioning from him in a workshop called *The Marketing Seminar*. He later shared these ideas in his book *This Is Marketing*. Essentially, positioning is about picking edges. The world we live in has an abundance of choices and options and a limited supply of time. A great way to stand out is therefore to pick some edges. By doing so you take a stand. Schools should consider this from a programmatic level. We know we can't be all things to all people. Those who try fail miserably. My other mentor, Aaron Walker, says, "Would you rather be a mile wide and an inch deep, or an inch wide and a mile deep?"

Picking edges acts as a magnet. It attracts the right kind of people and repels the wrong kind. When building the mastermind I had a number of edges to choose from:

Free	Expensive
Weekly	Monthly (or quarterly)
Face-to-face	Digitally
Read books in education	Read books outside of education
Safe	Experimental
Relaxed	Serious
Open	Reserved

There are no wrong edges. They are merely a signal of what you've built for who you serve. For example, in the masterminds I facilitate, I want to attract leaders who want to be open versus reserved. This is something that sets us apart from districts where leaders don't feel like they can be transparent. For whatever reason they may not feel safe, but if they aren't open about both their strengths and weaknesses, how will they ever get the help they need in order to grow?

When you pick an edge, you decide to stand for something, and whatever that something is, it matters a lot to who you serve. Whether it is a book, a mastermind, or a school, picking an edge is a great way to show what you are all about. It takes courage to pick an edge, but the benefits far outweigh the costs.

The mastermind core values are memorable. When I teach school leaders to create core values for themselves and their organizations, the key component is that they're sticky. Too many organizations create a vision, mission, and core values that are anything but sticky. They're vanilla and uninspiring. In contrast, sticky core values are remarkable because people remark on them. If a core value spreads by word of mouth, you've done your job as a leader. Sticky core values are unique to your organization. Nobody else has them.

How many schools claim core values like integrity, equity, and excellence? These are great ideals, but terrible values.

A sticky core value develops the story of the value. It tells everyone who hears the story *why the core value matters*. I promise, if you develop core values the sticky way, you create a clear path forward for your team. These core values are unambiguous. They tell the entire community, "We are proud that we show up like this."

In Season 1, Episode 169 of the *Better Leaders Better Schools* podcast, I was joined by Scott Long, a member of the Guiding Principals mastermind cohort. A proud Michigander and baseball enthusiast, Scott latched on to the idea of sticky core values. I love promoting stories of leaders who listen to the podcast and take action on an idea I present. Scott brought the sticky core values idea to his staff at Doherty Elementary.[48] The end result was sticky core values that were remarkable

---

[48] Scott wrote a detailed story on how he implemented this idea. The printed version is available on the companion website for this book, found at https://betterleadersbetterschools.com/master mindbook. You can also listen to our conversation on this topic by going to Season 1, Episode 169. The title is "How One Listener Took Massive Action for Incredible Results."

and provided clarity for the community based on who they are and what they want to be known for. Doherty Elementary also experienced tremendous pride in what they created because (a) it was a collaborative project and (b) they realized they accomplished something special.

Here is where they landed:

- All hands in

- Find your marigold

- Rocky's cuff links

- Respect

What's in a name? Those sticky core values definitely do the job of piquing the reader's interest and wanting to know more. When comparing Doherty's values with your school's values, which are more inspiring and authentic?

Creating a professional development experience that is authentic and nurtures authenticity is paramount to making real change in education. Imagine if Pablo Picasso decided he wanted to paint like Vincent van Gogh. It wouldn't have worked. The world needed both artists to create in a way aligned with their unique skills and vision. Leadership is also art, and the school leaders who learn to show up authentically because of psychological safety, high self-awareness, and being values-driven are on their way to maximizing their impact.

Authenticity is the first building block to the mastermind. The next reason our members soar is because of the sense of belonging they experience within our community.

Mastermind Case Study

Eugene Park

Principal at Russell Knight Elementary

What does a typical workday look like for you?

Well, typical, it's contextual, right? Typical right now in the midst of a pandemic and leading. Being a leader in a time of such uncertainty and things not being very clear when you try to look at what the future holds. I find that I'm spending a significant amount of time just clearly communicating to our community families as well as our teachers to keep them abreast of the changes that are taking place and also why a district or a building is making good decisions. I also find that during this time it's really pushed me to be even a better listener and communicator. There are a lot of opinions and concerns and feedback coming, and to be able to process that effectively, to be able to make sure that people feel heard, even if they don't get the decision that they want, really is crucial during this time.

I would say as a principal, the more I've been in the principalship, the more I feel like my number one purpose is to serve children. But I believe that the longer I've been a principal, I find that really my most important relationship is to ensure that kids get the best, to serve my teachers and my staff. Right now you're called to do a lot of blocking, right? You're called to do a lot of blocking for folks, providing time and support for them to adjust to this new way of working and being there for them. And so that's what I would say the principalship looks like right now, but generally speaking my message is pretty simple. We are a service-oriented profession. I believe as a principal, you should be the lead servant, and my message to myself and to my staff is to always seek to serve each other as well as the children that we have the privilege to care for. In a nutshell, I would say that is the job of the principalship, to serve others.

(Continued)

(Continued)

How has the mastermind helped you as a principal?

The mastermind has been an amazing experience. It's kind of crazy that I had never heard about it. Probably like three years ago, I think I heard Danny on a podcast talking about it. I can't remember, it might've been Jennifer Gonzalez, but I was very intrigued by and interested in it. I joined the mastermind and it really, truly has been the best professional development and professional cohort that I've been able to find really anywhere. In my twenty years in education, this is by far the best professional development experience that I've had as a teacher or as a principal. Something that is important to emphasize is the fact that I think a lot of folks, maybe some in general, might have really good connections at work as a principal and cohorts within their district or in the area.

But I think that's few. I think a lot of people have huge benefits in the mastermind. My experience is different in that I have an unbelievably strong network within my district, very supportive central staff. I have twelve elementary principals that I work extremely closely with and I would even consider many of them friends before colleagues. I have a great network, even in my setting, and yet joining the mastermind gives me a very different experience in that it avoids the groupthink. We (as in Cherry Hill "we") are used to certain things and how things are done and to be able to be in a group with people from Australia, people from other parts of the country, people from different districts and different experiences allows me to hear how people are working through the issues within the cohort that I have now in Cherry Hill. So even though I have an incredibly strong network I've found that the mastermind has allowed me to level up and even bring that to my close network here at home in Cherry Hill.

What do you think is the best part of the mastermind?

That's a hard one. I think I've benefited in different ways with all parts. I really enjoy it. I do enjoy the parts of it, like the books have been huge for me, and then having discussions and the push from the group to apply that and share how we're applying has been really powerful for me. I've always been a reader, at least within my professional career. I think I've grown in my ability to apply because there's an accountability piece, and I also love the hot seat. The hot seat is one of my favorite things to be a part of whether I'm on the hot seat or whether I am one of the people listening in and asking questions. I think it allows you to grow when you're on the hot seat. It allows you to become more vulnerable and know how to provide insights as to what you're going through or what you're thinking clearly so that people can ask questions and give you feedback. But then the other end, when you're the listener, it's really helped me to develop my ability to listen more effectively, to ask relevant questions, and to draw out the person on the hot seat, which I believe are really important.

I'm not sure if this is exactly what you're asking, but one of the best things for me, we as human beings are built to be in community. The fact that you meet every week, you might think, "Oh, it's virtual; you can't establish these meaningful relationships," and I found that to be completely false. I've developed really amazing relationships with folks. These are folks who you can be open with and vulnerable with, and really get input from them to help you to be better. Again, the added value of a mastermind, rather than just my cohort of Cherry Hill principals, is there's a benefit to not working in the same district as your colleagues, when you seek out input and feedback.

What's one way that the mastermind helped you approach leadership differently?

I've shared this before. Some of the things that have really, really recently had a significant impact on me have been Objectives and Key Results (OKRs) from *Measure What Matters* (Doerr, 2018). That idea has really had a significant impact on me as an individual in regards to really refining my goals, as I believe it's made me a better leader,

(Continued)

(Continued)

and that trickles down to my staff as well. That's something that's been really powerful for me. *Radical Candor* (Scott, 2019) has had a significant impact on me as well, and the way that I'm dialoguing with my staff and the way that I'm trying to build a culture with a lot of new people coming in. I'm not about brutal truths that can just be painful. I do believe in this radical candor, this idea that we can have a culture where people are open and honest and willing to push people and not feel afraid to be upfront in order to make each other better. Those are two things that have been really helpful to me recently that I can think of right off the top of my head.

What advice would you give a leader considering joining the mastermind?

I would say if you're looking to get better and to grow, I don't think you could find anything better. I would say, yes, it's helped me to become a better leader, but I'm a believer that you can't wear different masks. Yes, you act differently sometimes in a different context, but you are who you are at your core. I found that the mastermind has not only helped me to be a better leader, but I genuinely believe it's helping me to be a better person and therefore a better husband and a better father and a better leader within my church organization. I would say if you want to be better, not just as a leader, but as a person; if you want to stretch yourself, you truly want to grow because it takes work to do this work, I would join a mastermind. You won't regret it.

Anything else you'd like to say about the mastermind?

I can tell you that when I signed up in January, I was thinking, "Oh, I'll check it out for a year. It'll be nice. It'll be something different. I haven't really loved the PD that I've gotten thus far. Often it's $2,500 to go to one PD session for like a week and then it's over. What I found is I thought I would be there for a year and now I'm moving on within the mastermind and it has, it continues to just help me to grow and be better.

Chapter 3 Reflection Questions

Think of a professional development experience where you felt safe. How was it intentionally designed to foster a feeling of safety?

Consider your emotional intelligence. Even without taking an assessment, do you think you have stronger internal or external competence? How would you like to grow?

The stories we tell ourselves matter. Are there any stories that need revision (or deletion) because they do not serve you as a leader?

What are your core values that guide your leadership? Which are easy to adhere to? Which are more difficult to implement consistently and/or what gets in the way?

Do you already journal? What have you learned about yourself by journaling? What trends do you see and what needs to be addressed? If you don't already journal, what would it take to start today?

4 Belonging

///

Shared Purpose

"People like us do things like this."

−Seth Godin

Leadership Is for the Birds

The mastermind is like a murmuration, which is another name for a flock of starling birds. Murmuration also describes how the birds fly. Starlings have an uncanny and beautiful way of flying through the sky. You probably have seen it even if you are new to the word *murmuration*. Starlings are the birds that fly together, and at a moment's notice, the entire flock changes direction in unison. From a distance it seems as if the individual birds actually make up one big living organism.

How do hundreds, sometimes thousands, of starlings move as one in the sky?

According to Young et al. (2013), the starlings keep their focus narrow within the group, paying attention to six or seven other birds instead of the whole flock. Since each starling does this, they are able to move in unison as one large body.

I like the murmuration as a metaphor for the mastermind. A murmuration twists and turns throughout the sky, yet it moves as one and does not leave any starlings behind. The flexibility of the murmuration also means that there is equality and that everyone at some point can be the leader. One bird decides to move and the rest follow. A nice idea is to keep a small number of relationships very deep, which allows for greater connection to the entire community. Our entire community is large, but the smaller cohorts are where the magic happens.

Young et al. (2013) also note that starlings have "remarkable ability to maintain cohesion as a group in highly uncertain environments and with limited, noisy information"—a nice description of what goes on in a murmuration—and "when uncertainty in sensing is present, interacting with six or seven neighbors optimizes the balance between group cohesiveness and individual effort."

This description also leaves us a hint to why the mastermind works. School leadership occurs in a VUCA environment; it is volatile, uncertain, complex, and often ambiguous. Our leaders succeed because of the connection to a larger network of innovative leaders while forming intense relationships within a limited number of people in a cohort. We also avoid the "shiny object syndrome." Calm voices and clear heads help leaders focus on what is most important and ignore the noise that exists in the world.

This metaphor works, but leaders are not birds. If you want to create more powerful professional development experiences and help school administrators take their leadership to the next level, the key is to focus on shared purpose.

For or With?

The *Harvard Business Review* article "Purpose Is Good. Shared Purpose Is Better" compares a number of company mission statements to drive home a point. The gist of the article is that businesses need to move from creating purpose that is *for* who they serve to creating purpose *with* those they serve.

> Customers are no longer just consumers; they're co-creators. They aren't just passive members of an audience; they are active members of a community. They want to be a part of something; to belong; to influence; to engage. It's not enough that they feel good about your purpose. They want it to be their purpose too. They don't want to be at the other end of your "for." They want to be right there with you. Purpose needs to be shared. (Bonchek, 2013)

School leaders (customers) engage in (consume) professional development, which is usually created with a desire to help them. The professional development is created for them. Come to this workshop. Take this online course. Graduate from "X" University and earn your principal's licensure.

Powerful professional development is different. Belonging is at the center of the design. In the mastermind, our focus is creating the experience *with* the leaders we serve.

Mission statements tell us who you are, what you do, and why you do it. To illustrate his point on shared purpose, Bonchek uses business mission statements.

> Adidas: The Adidas Group strives to be the global leader in the sporting goods industry with brands built on a passion for sports and a sporting lifestyle (Bonchek, 2013).

> Nike: To bring inspiration and innovation to every athlete* in the world.

---

* If you have a body, you are an athlete (Bonchek, 2013).

How do you respond to each mission statement? Which one is more welcoming? Which invites you to belong? Which inspires you?[48]

Although I love wearing Adidas myself, I have to admit that Nike's mission is incredible. Even when I look down at my stomach and there is no evidence of six-pack abs, Nike inspires me to work out. I am an athlete. I belong to the "athlete" tribe, and I don't have to play for a professional sport club to believe that about myself.

Shared purpose is powerful like that. It connects us and makes us experience belonging. Professional development with this design aim in mind creates experiences that are far better than those that are merely created for school administrators.

Another way we build shared purpose in the mastermind is through agreements. Next, we will learn what agreements are and how they are different from expectations.[49] Then, we will walk through the agreements that exist within the mastermind.

Why Agreements Are Better Than Expectations

When I was learning to be a coach and mastermind facilitator, I invested in as many books, courses, and conferences as I could find. At some point I came across the great work of an expert coach named Steve Chandler. He is one of the best coaches in the world and has a unique perspective on "Expectation vs. Agreement." This philosophy deeply guided how the mastermind was created, and I adapted his teaching for the context of school.

---

[48] Could your school's mission use a refresher? Is it done for your students, staff, and community, or is it done with?
[49] I consider expectations a dirty word. I hope you will agree with me based on what I share in the next section.

According to Chandler (2015), agreements are better than expectations.

How do you motivate and influence the people in your school?

Expectations are shared by a principal to their staff—Here is what I expect you to do (by this date) . . . And this is what a quality job looks like . . .

Agreements are co-created with stakeholders to define what needs to happen by when. Often, how the work is done isn't necessarily defined, but it could be.

Expectations fall short of motivating others because they

- Are toxic

- Ruin chances at a good relationship

- See everything as a problem (job performance, quality standards, etc.)

- Are stressful

- Are ridden with anxiety

- Are reactive

- Are fear-based

- Are cowardly

People resent expectations. That's because they are often unrealistic and out-of-touch (Chandler, 2015, pp. 109–129).

Is there anything worse than an out-of-touch, unrelatable leader?

My working theory of leadership is that leadership is service. That's impossible to accomplish if you're out-of-touch. Think back for a minute to a boss who really drove you nuts. Would you say they understood you and the context of your work?

When I was a teacher, if I had a principal who needed "X" task completed on an unreasonable timeline or just expected something I could never deliver, no amount of expectations would change my effort or my ability to deliver. And worse yet, I would lose more respect for that leader (if I had any left). Don't let that be you. Think about it. Have you ever heard or (worse) said any of these phrases?

> *"If it wasn't for my staff, we would just be able to do _____."*

> *"_____ task needs to be done by [unreasonable time] or else."*

> *"They should know how to do _____; I sent them an email."*

> *"I don't want to hold their hand; they are a 'professional.'"*

The problem with expectations and these kinds of phrases is that they set you up for failure. Expectations are a path to disappointment, or at best, a neutral experience. Consider this—if your staff doesn't meet your expectations, then how will you feel? Disappointed.

If your staff *does* meet your expectations, how will you feel? Neutral.

> "Well, Danny, they're just doing what I expected."

People do not look forward to meeting your expectations. In fact, they rebel against them.

The solution is agreements. People love to keep co-authored agreements. They are much more powerful.

According to Chandler (2015), agreements are

- Co-authored

- Creative

- Courageous

- Motivating

- Win–win

- Generous

- Momentous

- Culture building (pp. 109–129)

Think of the following scenario in a fictitious school.

Principal: *We need to cut the absence rate of seniors by 30 percent by the end of the month.*

AP: *Well . . . I can't promise that by the end of the month.*

Principal: *What do you mean?*

AP: *Well, we have no interventions set up, no budget for incentives or bus passes, and to be honest, we don't have a compelling reason for seniors to get to school. I think if we could offer some PD to our staff regarding positive behavioral interventions and supports [PBIS] and create some type of challenge with prizes for the seniors who improve their attendance the most, then I think we could make a significant dent in our attendance problem. But I'll need some time to plan, time with teachers, and a budget for incentives/prizes. If I had that, we could improve attendance in thirty days. If not, I don't see us moving the needle much at all.*

Principal: *Hmm . . . let me think . . . I can give you next Wednesday with the entire staff to discuss PBIS and to develop a compelling project that would excite seniors and drive engagement. I'll also give you $1,000 to get prizes to provide to seniors as incentives. If I do that, can you agree to improve our attendance by the end of the month?*

AP: *I believe I could deliver on that.*

Principal: *Great. Let's get started. Let me know if you need anything else from me or if you anticipate any problems with this project.*

So if agreements are stronger than expectations, why, then, do most leaders walk around with only expectations?

The challenge: Sit down with your staff next week. Ask them what they really need to get the job done. Allow them to ask questions and ask for the help they need to deliver on their word.

People love to keep agreements they helped create.

As a bonus, you get to find out in advance why certain things (including problems) occur and how to navigate through them before they even happen.

Imagine if you could predict why a plan might fail and address it before it even happens. That's another advantage of agreements that you just won't get from expectations.

If you accept this challenge, get ready for something magical to happen within your organization. You also get to experience the freedom of leading without the resentment of staff not living up to your expectations.

Be brave. Be courageous.

Be creative and do the hard work of negotiating agreements with your people. Yes, I guarantee it's harder than walking around with a bunch of high expectations. But I also guarantee you'll go a lot further. Not in the short term, but in the long term. And that's okay. Education isn't a sprint, is it?

It's a marathon.

You can choose right now—do you want a life of disappointment, or at best a neutral, "they-met-my-expectations" experience? Or would you like the magic, wonder, and results that you will drive when you play in the realm of courageous agreements?

The choice is clear to me. I hope the choice is clear for you as well. Up next are the agreements we created within the mastermind.

Mastermind Agreements

After working in the mastermind for just over a year, I drafted the following agreements for the mastermind to review:

- We picked you to be you.

- Give yourself (and others) an A.

- Generosity. Always.

- Show up. We're better together. We need your voice.

- Assume positive intent.

- Be creative and experiment.

- We avoid hot button issues.

- Make a ruckus.

- Ripple effect.

They were based on the natural ways we had been gathering. My goal was to capture what seemed to make our community work. With a draft in hand, we engaged in a process where we read through the agreements and made edits where necessary. Some agreements were deleted completely. Some were birthed out of this process. Most were a work in progress and then received a stamp of approval.

Over the next few sections, I will share the actual definition of each agreement.

We picked you to be you.

The first agreement is, "We picked you to be you." Don't try to be anyone else.

You are a wonder. No one else in this world has had the same experiences as you've had. You have much to add. Your perspective matters and when you share it, we all get better. Don't try to be anyone else. Be you.

This is an important agreement. It's easy for humans to get into the comparison game, but that never serves us well. Some of my most spectacular failures were when I tried to be someone else. Once as a sixth-grade teacher at East Cobb Middle School in Marietta, Georgia, I tried to have my students line up in a row absolutely silent before entering my classroom. I stole the idea from an eighth-grade history teacher who previously served in the military. He brought that experience to his classroom and I was amazed at how the toughest kids in the school wouldn't utter a peep before entering the class or while working at their desk. And when I tried to do that it was an epic failure. I don't even know *why* I tried to emulate this teacher.

I prefer a classroom where there is high energy and loads of collaboration. It's no wonder when I tried his approach it didn't work. What I learned from this experience is the importance of being me. Looking back, I hadn't yet mastered my confidence in giving control to students. I knew this was the right approach; I was handing the reins to my class and helping them take ownership of their learning. I thought this would be how Paulo Freire would teach, yet I still measured my success as a teacher against my eighth-grade social studies colleague. I lacked the confidence to say that my process could be messy, would sometimes fail, but would inspire kids to take their learning to a whole new level because they were in charge.

I want new members in the mastermind to know that we are absolutely thrilled that they signed up, and that we all will benefit when they bring what makes them unique to our community.

One of my mentors, Derek Sivers, says, "What is ordinary to you is extraordinary to me."

What a great reminder that what we do is amazing and will benefit others when we show up and share.

Give yourself (and others) an A.

This agreement originates in my number one favorite book of all time, *The Art of Possibility* by Rosamund Stone Zander and Benjamin Zander. In the book are twelve practices that will enhance your life, leadership, and creativity. One of these practices is "Give an A."

Here is how I describe it to new members:

> There are no grades in the mastermind, but if there were, it would be an A. And guess what . . . you already have an A. There is nothing you can do to earn or lose that A. This is not a place where we compete. It is not a tryout. We're all equals here.

It can be intimidating to join a community of high-performing leaders (even when you are already one). Everyone struggles with imposter syndrome, and some members wonder how they will ever measure up—which builds on the first agreement: be yourself.

It's important that everyone knows not only do we accept them for who they are, but we believe they are an absolute wonder! Part of my philosophy of leadership is if I radically love and care for the leaders I serve, then they will leave meetings inspired, equipped, encouraged, and motivated to go and serve their communities at an even higher level. This helps us live out our purpose: *Everyone wins when a leader gets better. Everyone wins when you get better.*

There is also a sigh-of-relief moment when new members realize that we don't compete in this space. We build up and encourage. I have been fortunate enough to build a space where individuals are on equal footing, which allows us to experiment, take risks, and push each other to grow.

Many leaders already put a lot of pressure on themselves to do their best, but working to be the best or earn an "A" has a nasty side effect. The unintended consequence is that you play it safe because you are worried about how you will be seen and evaluated. In the worst scenarios, you may try to bring down others so that you can hold the only spot at the top.

In the mastermind, everyone gets an A and there is plenty of space for you at the top. This is different from a seventh-place trophy, which I don't believe in. I still challenge and encourage excellence in everything mastermind members do, but we make an effort to take the evaluative aspect of performance in leadership.

Generosity. Always.

Generosity. Always. Ask yourself, "What is the most generous thing I can do today?" and then go do that. If you have something you want to say, but you're nervous . . . Say it. Someone else might be thinking the same thing. We are a give-to-give community. Consider how you can help others level up (Bauer, 2020).

This is the only way to exist in the mastermind. Earlier in the book I referred to Adam Grant's work that explored "givers and takers" and how we only want givers in the mastermind. A generous spirit is how members behave.

I like this agreement because the focus is other-centric rather than ego-centric. It's not about me and it's not about you. It is about how we can help others be the best version of themselves.

Too often we keep great ideas to ourselves, sometimes because we are selfish, but other times because we judged the ideas as unworthy and filed them away before giving them a chance. I love pointing out an elephant in the room or asking the simplest question. These innocent observations have great value because usually they put language to something *everyone else is thinking* or they extend permission to others to be authentic and speak what is on their mind.

Show up. We're better together. We need your voice.

One thing I want to be crystal clear about in the mastermind is the importance of the community itself. All of us are better than any of us. This agreement reads:

> Show up. We're better together. We need your voice. This builds on the idea that "we picked you to be you." If you're not around, we miss out. People are investing their money, time, and emotional labor to grow within the mastermind. When you're not there we miss out (Bauer, 2020).

My friend JB says, "You can't make up real life." Of course there will be times when family or the job conflicts with making a mastermind meeting. What I want this agreement to communicate is that we all are better when members are consistent in attendance. The value of networking with other high performers is the level of discourse and feedback offered within the group. If members were sparsely attending, then there would be little point in gathering.

I'm sure some people enjoy working closely with me, but that quickly shifts to desiring to connect with other mastermind members at the same time and place each week. Members are literally paying to hear what others think on the different topics and hot seat questions we discuss. There is no formal percentage of attendance I ask members to agree to. I do keep attendance to keep myself accountable for knowing if someone is consistently out. That usually means they need help. What I have found is that when people need to lean in to the mastermind the most, they hide. When life is tough, some leaders think they can't spare the hour to gather, but they couldn't be further from the truth. The point of the mastermind is to empower members and encourage them. Leaders leave our gatherings excited to do the work, but when leadership is especially tough it can be easier to hide.

Assume positive intent.

Not only will you be so much happier, I think leadership is much easier when you assume positive intent. The world and life are already tough enough. It isn't very useful to look around the room and believe that other people have it out for us and are working intently to sabotage our good efforts.

Assume positive intent. This will be a better community if we believe everyone is doing the best they can with what they know. Let's assume they have positive intent (Bauer, 2020).

A less generous spin on this agreement is a mental model called Hanlon's Razor, which simply states that we should not attribute to malice what can be explained by stupidity. This mental model reminds us that people do make mistakes, and not all negative results are due to the scheming of an evil genius.

If we choose to believe that people are doing the best they can with what they know, our approach in leadership is lighter, more positive, and more optimistic. We are flexible and able to stay curious by thinking, "I wonder why that happened? What can I learn from this experience?" as opposed to negatively judging the actions of another when their actions do not benefit or, worse, harm us.

A great book that examines how leaders can stay curious is called *Change Your Questions, Change Your Life* by Marilee Adams. This is one of the best books on leadership and coaching I have ever read. The big idea Adams presents in the book is "The Choice Map," which essentially categorizes all events a leader experiences into two potential paths. The "Judger Path" is characterized by automatic reactions, is blame focused, and places individuals in a win–lose relationship. The better path for leaders is the "Learner Path," which is characterized by thoughtful choices, is solution-focused, and offers a win–win relationship to individuals (Adams, 2009).

The beautiful thing about "The Choice Map" is inherent in the name. When we find ourselves on the "Judger Path" we can switch lanes at any time by asking learner questions. This is the essence of a curious leader and helps us assume positive intent before mistakenly and unhelpfully assigning blame.

Be creative and experiment.

I took the altMBA, an alternative MBA program from Seth Godin, in the winter of 2019. It was a transformational experience, and the program noticed the work I put in. As a result, they invited me to be a coach, and a year later, I applied for a head coach position.

> If we choose to believe that people are doing the best they can with what they know, our approach in leadership is lighter, more positive, and more optimistic.

I'll never forget coming to the head coach training. I was surrounded by the best-of-the-best coaches. My coach as a student was the brilliant Irishman Conor McCarthy. When I went through the head coach training, there, too, was Conor. Everywhere I looked, I saw someone who was ten times more talented than myself.

Being competitive and wanting to "land" the head coach position, my mind shifted into compete mode. This is at times a strength and at other times a liability. In the middle of coming up with my strategy to win, the provost of the altMBA, Marie, uttered five very important words that changed everything for me: "This is not a tryout."

I let out a long exhale. My shoulders relaxed. My jaw loosened. I was in the right place, but more importantly, I now embodied a more helpful coaching posture—one of creativity, curiosity, and flexibility.

Many schools suffer from doublespeak. They want to encourage innovation and risk-taking. They espouse being a place where it's "okay to fail." Schools want to be cutting edge like Silicon Valley tech start-ups, but unfortunately their actions say something quite different.

Whack! The proverbial 2 × 4 cracks across the skull of a school leader who put themselves out there, only to find out that the idea of innovation was meant for coffee mugs and the district website, not for actual implementation when it came to curriculum and instruction, discipline, or the actual structure of the school building.

The mastermind is different. We want our members to be creative and experiment. There is no better place to support this kind of innovation than in a think tank of peers who will provide critical feedback and take fledgling ideas and make them stronger before we bring them to the larger staff and supervisors when the stakes are high.

This is how our mastermind agreement reads on this subject:

> Be creative and experiment. If you already "have an A" and know that we aren't competing with one another, then how would you show up? How can you be wildly creative and experiment within the mastermind? What would you do if anything was possible? What would you do if you knew no one would judge you? (Bauer, 2020).

Although it can be a challenge to surround yourself with other world-class leaders and take risks, those who do find their way to breakthroughs. This consistently occurs in the space of a mastermind because we give an A and are creative and experiment.

We avoid hot button issues.

Many school leaders decide that they get enough support from other leaders on social media. In my view, these leaders are substituting busyness and occasional value for deep work and dramatic growth. Worse yet, social media gives everyone a microphone, even those who obviously don't deserve a seat at the table. Racists, sexists, and trolls are far too common. Less egregious are the constant complainers, and this is why I've dubbed social media as the new toxic faculty lounge.[50]

---

[50] Funny story—at my first teaching job at East Cobb Middle in Marietta, Georgia, I went to get a refill of coffee in the faculty lounge. The middle school was huge. Almost 2000 kids in sixth to eighth grade. During the first week, I hadn't come close to meeting all the staff. So there I was, getting some coffee, and one of my elder colleagues asked to see my student ID. I couldn't believe it and told her that I was a teacher. I've had a beard nearly all my adult life.

As an undergraduate student preparing to become an educator, my professor wisely encouraged me to avoid the faculty lounge.

"Why?" I wondered.

She gently explained that in too many schools, the lounge was a place where teachers went to complain and gossip, rarely moving the conversation forward or doing anything meaningful for students. My experiences in the faculty room confirmed what my professor taught me, and social media is the new place for many negative-minded people to congregate and gossip.

We avoid hot button issues and whining because they trigger unproductive conversations. That is the antithesis of the mastermind. We solve problems. We level up. We are solution-oriented (Bauer, 2020).

On the positive side, social media is a great place to make initial connections, nurture relationships, and share resources, but because of the artificial nature of tech, it cannot be transformational. For that, you need humans and connection.

Put boundaries and time limits on engaging in social media and then find opportunities to go deep with peers in a setting like a mastermind.

Make a ruckus.

A Ruckus Maker is first and foremost an innovative leader, but after that, they make change happen in education.

So either I was clean-shaven with a baby face and tall for a middle schooler or some of our middle school students shouldn't have been retained so long if they were showing up to eighth grade with a full beard!

This is how I refer to both listeners of the *Better Leaders Better Schools* podcast as well as members in the mastermind. We attract those out-of-the-box thinkers who, in their current setting, may think, "Am I crazy? Am I the only one who thinks we could do this?"

It doesn't surprise me anymore when new members join and tell me how they thought they were the only one who thought this way. To meet others who want to push education further in different ways is a life-transforming event. It emboldens leaders and encourages them to create the change they want to see in the world for the benefit of their students.

Leadership is isolating and tough enough doing it the traditional way. To be a Ruckus Maker and create change on your own is nearly impossible. The mastermind exists to connect, support, encourage, and equip our members.

I often tell them, "You can't pour from an empty cup."

The mastermind is a time just for school leaders. Where else does this happen in their life? Everywhere else they have to be "on" and giving. After all, leadership is service. The mastermind is a unique place where leaders can let their guard down and receive support and nourishment in their profession.

I invest in a mastermind, coaching, and conferences so I can give my best to the leaders I serve. They, in turn, have an abundance to pour out from in order to serve their communities. It's a benevolent circle that continues to give as long as we take care of ourselves first.

Ripple effect.

Everything we do in the mastermind is about paying it forward. Nothing brings me greater satisfaction than when I hear how a member took an idea and used it in their community with great success. A number of masterminds in education have started from the one we began at Better Leaders Better Schools, and I haven't come across a mastermind in education that I didn't help start.

That's the point of this book. It's to tell district and local school leaders that this kind of high-quality professional development exists. You don't have to lead alone. That's a choice.

The mastermind experience is powerful professional development because it's built on the ABCs. Take the ideas and implement them on your own. Contact me and I'll guide you through the process. Or simply jump in to a running and well-oiled machine like the masterminds we offer at Better Leaders Better Schools.

This is how I describe the ripple effect.

Steal what you learn here in the mastermind. Make it your own. Then make your community better. Our members regularly use ideas we model during mastermind meetings within their own community. Some members have even started internal masterminds (Bauer, 2020).[51]

Like a stone that is dropped into the calm water, ripples emerge and carry out that energy far past the initial point of contact. We can transform education with this one simple idea and approach to serving school leaders.

---

[51] Let's cause a ripple effect together. Be the first reader to buy this book for ten colleagues and I will personally coach you each week for a month for free. Send your proof of purchase to daniel@better leadersbetterschools.com.

What's in a Name?

Agreements create a sense of belonging. Group names are another powerful way to foster belonging as well. The BLBS community is the Ruckus Makers, and within each cohort, members have decided on the name as well. It was fun to put this challenge to each group. I gave them ten minutes or so to discuss, debate, and come to consensus on a group name during one meeting years ago. The cohorts have since been called No Pockets, Purple Cows, Free Spirits, and Guiding Principals.

Names have meaning. They are our identity. Just like sticky core values, there is a story behind each name. These stories I will share next in order to inspire you and show what is possible.

No Pockets. One day, Kyle, a principal in Texas, asked the rest of the group what female principals do to carry their keys, IDs, radio, and so on. As a male leader, I didn't even think of the challenge that female leaders face. We have suits with pockets in our jackets. Our pants always have pockets.[52] What I learned that night is that female professional wardrobe options *rarely* have pockets. That's maybe less of a big deal as a corporate executive who might have an assistant or "handler" who carries stuff for you. But as a principal, this is a big deal. And that is how this cohort got its name.

Purple Cows. Not only is this a great book by Seth Godin, but it's also the name of a particularly zany group of masterminders. I used to drive the two-and-a-half-hour route from Chicago to the University of Illinois campus down I-57 countless times during my

---

[52] Although cargo pants took that a bit too far in my opinion. I loved cargo pants as a young bachelor in college and after college. This is probably the sole reason I was a bachelor at the time. Once I emotionally matured in my thirties, I said goodbye to my cargo pants and then started regularly getting dates!

undergraduate and graduate years. Between the urban landscape of a sprawling city and the Illinois campus, there are a lot of cornfields and a lot of cows. There are brown-spotted cows. And there are black-spotted cows. There are no purple-spotted cows. If there were, it would be certainly remarkable, and that is what it means to be a "purple cow." It means creating something that is so interesting people talk about it and spread the idea by word of mouth. This group's identity reflects the kind of work they set out to do on their campuses—purple-cow-type work.

Free Spirits. Like the name, this is a very independent and creative group. There are traditional leaders, out-of-the-box leaders, and then free spirits—leaders who don't even realize there is a box to begin with. Their name is also a play on the word "spirit." It's not uncommon for a member to show up with a glass of wine or pint of beer. Imagine that—professional development where you can have a drink![53]

Guiding Principals. This cohort wanted to pick a serious name that reflected the principles that they live by. In Chapter 3, you learned how living in alignment with your values is one aspect of being an authentic leader. This group is the epitome of leading in alignment with their values. Since they are also school leaders, they

---

[53] After all, everyone is an adult. Plus, why not? I remember when I first moved to Belgium. After dropping our luggage in our new home, my wife and I set off to find some breakfast. We were hungry after the international flight. While waiting for our breakfast and enjoying our coffee, I had to rub my eyes because I couldn't believe what I saw. There in the plaza was an older gentleman having his breakfast and a beer while reading the Het Krant (The Newspaper). "How fascinating!" I thought. The best part of living around the world is having your worldview expand. A beer at 8 a.m. in Antwerp, Belgium, is completely normal. It doesn't mean you are an alcoholic. It means you are Belgian. Beer is actually cheaper than water at many of the restaurants there. Fascinating indeed! So a beer at professional development seems perfectly okay to me. Stuffy leaders need not apply to the mastermind.

decided to also play with the idea of "principle" and switch that to "principal."

Shared purpose can be built by naming cohorts of a mastermind or using co-created agreements that leaders commit to live by. Another great way to build belonging into professional development is by creating inclusive environments, which we will look at next.

Mastermind Case Study
Shbrone Brookings
Principal at Ralph Downs Elementary

"After joining the mastermind, I possess an instantly attainable network of global resources."

Tell us what you do and what your work typically entails.

I'm an elementary principal in Oklahoma City, where I get the opportunity to create a positive educational environment with a focus on learning, growth, and overall success. I love my job. My daily work entails making decisions that impact the lives of our students and teachers. I attempt to see the brilliance in others and encourage them to see it in themselves. My desire is for everyone in my school to feel respected and connected.

How has the mastermind helped you?

The mastermind provides engaging and impactful gatherings with world-class educators. Within a short amount of time, we build strong relationships, share ideas and strategies, and support one another in various ways. Being inspired by the process, I have noticed that my building-level meetings and daily interactions with friends and family are much more intentional and meaningful.

(Continued)

(Continued)

What's the best part of the mastermind?

You are instantly surrounded by positive people where you can be vulnerable, affirmed, and challenged. Ideally, when I purposefully meet with colleagues, I like to leave feeling better than when I arrived. I consistently get that feeling every week. I believe my commitment to the mastermind is not just time spent but also an investment in my future.

What is one way the mastermind has helped you approach leadership differently?

I am much more proactive. As a school leader, I was typically reactive regarding new technology, techniques, and applications. I would usually wait for a few other people to test things out before I felt comfortable with any implementation. This community is composed of dynamic, cutting-edge risk-takers who have encouraged me to do the same. We regularly discuss tips and innovative ways to work more effectively and efficiently. I now have access to such an abundance of resources, and I currently do not hesitate to step out of my comfort zone and be the first in my district to spearhead new things.

What advice would you give a leader considering joining the mastermind?

Do it! It is a special place that will enable you to effectively learn, reflect, and level up as a leader.

Inclusive Environments

I celebrate myself,

And what I assume you shall assume,

For every atom belonging to me as good belongs to you.

–Walt Whitman, "Song of Myself"

Mismatched Environments

After graduating college, I took a road trip through the South. That spring I put my résumé out to anywhere warm, including California, Arizona, Georgia, Texas, the Carolinas, and Florida. I knew I was sick of snow and I was substituting the frigid winters of Midwest living for a warmer climate anywhere else. The West didn't respond to my résumé at all, but the Southeast did. After setting up a number of interviews, I jumped into a car with my friend Paul and we traveled from Champaign, Illinois, to Atlanta, Georgia. My first stop was in the East Cobb Middle School District in Marietta, Georgia.[54]

Paw prints lined the pavement on Holt Road. Wheeler High School was situated across the street from East Cobb Middle School. Both were home to "The Wild-cats." A few hours after my first official interview, I was offered my first teaching job.

Paul and I drove to Stone Mountain so we could get in a hike. There, 1686 feet above sea level, I called my favorite professor of all time, Dr. Arlette Willis.[55] We spoke about the job opportunity and the impact I could have. I accepted the job a few minutes later.

My mother was surprised I wasn't coming back to the Chicago suburbs to teach. She understood when I told

---

[54] Marietta is home to Cabbage Patch Dolls and an Air Force base. The home of Julia Roberts, Smyrna, was only a town or two away.

[55] At the time, I didn't realize the layers of race during that call. There I was standing on top of a racist monument. Stone Mountain has Confederate generals chiseled into the side of it and the Ku Klux Klan was known to actively parade through the streets there. And here I was speaking to my version of an education "Yoda," a Black woman who opened my eyes to privilege and impressed upon me the importance of social justice and multiculturalism. I would go on to teach in predominantly Black and Brown schools.

her, "Mom, those kids have plenty of good teachers. I am going to make a difference where I'm needed."

I share this story because, over my decades-long career as an educator, I found myself choosing as a white male to bring my talent to predominantly Black and Brown spaces. I do not regret this choice. But the fact that the majority of the teaching population doesn't reflect the culture of the students is something I think about often. Hansen and Quintero (2018) report from the American Community Survey that 75% of administrators and 80% of teachers are white; while only 50% of our students are white.

Gender Mismatch

Female leadership also is underrepresented in school administration even though women represent the majority of teachers. Superville (2017) found that women represent 76 percent of teachers, 52 percent of principals, and 78 percent of central-office administrators. However, women account for less than 25 percent of all superintendents. When it comes to leadership in the corporate sector, the trends are similar. DeHaas et al. (2019) found that white women represented 17.9 percent and minority women 4.6 percent of all board seats of Fortune 500 companies in 2018. Table 4.1 represents the percentage of women in corporate senior leadership around the world ("Women in Management," 2020).

Better Leaders Better Schools' mastermind cohorts represent the same trends we see when it comes to leaders of color (26 percent) and women in leadership (45 percent). As an industry, we must do better.

How do we do better? Jain-Link et al. (2020) share five strategies organizations can adopt to create an

Table 4.1   The Global Percentage of Women in
            Senior Leadership Positions

REGION	PERCENTAGE OF WOMEN IN SENIOR LEADERSHIP
Africa	38
Eastern Europe	35
Latin America	33
European Union	30
North America	29
Asia Pacific (APAC)	27

Source: Women in Management (2020).

inclusive workplace: emphasize the business case for diversity and inclusion, recognize bias, practice inclusive leadership, provide sponsorship programs, and hold leadership accountable.

In lieu of a business case, it makes sense to champion an inclusive environment in education. Whether it's Hansen and Quintero's (2018) work looking at the demographic mismatch in schools or Superville's (2017) research exploring women in educational leadership, our students need to see themselves reflected in school administration. Bond et al. (2015) found a number of benefits of a diverse teaching force, including the following:

- "Minority teachers can be more motivated to work with disadvantaged minority students in high-poverty, racially and ethnically segregated schools, a factor which may help to reduce rates of teacher attrition in hard-to-staff schools.

- Minority teachers tend to have higher academic expectations for minority students, which can result in increased academic and social growth among students.

- Minority students profit from having among their teachers individuals from their own racial and ethnic group who can serve as academically successful role models and who can have greater knowledge of their heritage culture.

- Positive exposure to individuals from a variety of races and ethnic groups, especially in childhood, can help to reduce stereotypes, attenuate unconscious implicit biases and help promote cross-cultural social bonding.

- All students benefit from being educated by teachers from a variety of different backgrounds, races and ethnic groups, as this experience better prepares them to succeed in an increasingly diverse society" (p. 1).

Recognizing bias is a more difficult proposition. It's nearly impossible in homogeneous groups. According to Duke (2019), "To get a more objective view of the world, we need an environment that exposes us to alternate hypotheses and different perspectives. That doesn't apply only to the world around us: to view *ourselves* in a more realistic way, we need other people to fill in our blind spots" (p. 138). The mastermind is an uncommon form of professional development that produces an uncommon yet powerful result. By intentionally selecting diverse members, we are able to limit the bias, conscious or not, from interfering with our leadership ability.

In Chapter 5, we will look at how we rotate facilitation in the mastermind. This is an essential component of "challenge" in the ABCs of powerful professional development™. But rotating leaders of the mastermind also creates an inclusive space and belonging. Demetrius Ball is a principal of a multicultural school in the San Francisco Bay area. A graduate of West Point and an ultra-marathoner, Demetrius brings a level of preparation and focus to the mastermind that is unique to him. During a mastermind meeting in January 2021, Demetrius opened in a way I have not seen yet. He shared a short, two-paragraph story that he read to us and we then discussed:

Jake is a construction manager that has lived in San Ramon with his wife and two children for 15 years. All of Jake's friends and neighbors look just like him and have very similar backgrounds. Jake spends most of his time at home and his job sites in Oakland and San Francisco. As a manager, Jake is responsible for hiring and supervising all of the hourly workers on his job sites. The majority of those workers are Latinx or Black. Jake gets really frustrated with his workers because he feels that many, not all, are unreliable because they often do not show up on time to the site. He has also noticed that many lack the basic math skills to be effective with fractions, an important skill for their work to be done properly.

One evening Jake and his wife, Amy, went out to eat at a Japanese steak house in

(Continued)

(Continued)

Walnut Creek and struck up a conversation with another couple sitting next to them, Isaiah and his wife Simone. The couples end up sharing stories about their families and hobbies. The two men find out that they were both diehard Warriors fans and discussed the glory of the championship Warriors. The conversation eventually turned to work, and Isaiah shared that he is an executive at an educational consulting firm. Jake felt comfortable enough with Isaiah to share his frustration with many of his hourly workers. Isaiah listened as Jake went into detail about how difficult it was to work with "those" people and how the education system was failing people from those neighborhoods. Isaiah seemed a little uncomfortable with the direction the conversation was heading, but he continued to entertain Jake. As the night came to a close and the couples exchanged their goodbyes, Jake proudly said to Isaiah, "I have a tremendous amount of respect for Black people like you who are educated and have made something of themselves." Isaiah and Simone quickly looked at each other, turned, and walked away without so much as a goodbye. (Ball, 2021)

I'm sure you can imagine the depth and quality of discussion we had following this story. Demetrius's mastermind cohort is filled with leaders from across the United States and includes a principal in Nepal. The schools represented are public, private, a Jewish day school, even a school on a Native American reservation. Having *these kinds* of discussions in a group as diverse as ours is exactly how you create an inclusive environment.

In researching this book, I was introduced to the idea of sponsorships, where novice leaders of color are paired with veteran leaders of color who can help them progress in their career and "learn the ropes." Eighty-one percent of women of color who had sponsors were more likely to be satisfied with their career progression versus their sponsorless peers (Jain-Link et al., 2020). As a white male, I must admit I didn't even consider this for the mastermind, but now that my eyes are open, I commit to building that into our onboarding process. Sponsorship opportunities say, "I see you and recognize your needs are different from those of your white peers." This is an easy win to make the mastermind even more inclusive and to foster a greater sense of belonging.

Leadership accountability is the final of five aspects that Jain-Link et al. (2020) suggest for creating inclusive environments. The mastermind is currently small enough that members have a direct line of communication with me. This helps hold me accountable for choices I make that impact the entire mastermind. Additionally, the agreements we looked at in the previous section value inclusion—specifically, "we picked you to be you." The spaces I occupy are usually diverse. The mastermind has to be. Gone unchecked, it's natural to build teams that are homogeneous in terms of belief, behavior, and ethnicity. Just like I did as a young teacher, I've built a community that is intentionally diverse. The agreement "we picked you to be you" challenges members to show up and bring their full identity to our group. The value "whole hearts and whole selves" does the same. One way leaders can be held accountable for building inclusive spaces is by building that into their core values (Jain-Link et al., 2020).

Books We Choose to Read

One way we *do better* is by engaging in conversations that need to happen. Around 2017, I asked mastermind members to challenge the traditions that exist in their schools. Many traditions are built for students, faculties, and communities that no longer exist and represent the reality of the school communities of today. Some traditions and policies are discriminatory and racist by design. This inspired me to question the traditions and culture at Better Leaders Better Schools. At the time, the organization was only two years old. My epiphany was this—if I care about diversity and inclusion, where did that show up in my work? At that point I made a more concerted effort to seek out guests on my podcast who represented diverse perspectives. I thought, "Do I even need to host my podcast?" Considering that question, I formed a *School Leadership Series* podcast team that was diverse. I provided support and training to a new team of podcast hosts and handed them the microphone. Building a platform that is respected in the podcast space and amplifying the diverse perspectives of the team has been some of the most rewarding work I've done in recent years. In the context of school leadership, a principal can work harder to build a diverse administrative team and faculty, as well as make sure voices that are underrepresented have a seat at the table on all school committees.

One blind spot I confronted with the help of the mastermind was that the majority of books we read and discussed were from a white male perspective. That was an easy fix. Now we include books that are written by female and BIPOC authors.[56] In addition to leader-

---

[56] In the Resources section, you will find not only a list of every book we've read in the mastermind since 2016, but also a list of books written by BIPOC authors. All of these books will push you as a leader.

ship topics like mindset, decision making, culture, and so on, we also read books that discuss race and equity from a high-level, cultural perspective. I take great pride that members have appreciated this effort, often noting, "I never would have read 'X' book. It changed my perspective and made me a better leader. Thank you, Danny."

Some Practical Tips

Inclusive environments are more expansive than gender and race. Making sure we invite the contribution and ideas of individual members is another consideration when creating belonging via inclusive environments. For the remainder of this section, I'll share a few intentional activities we do within the mastermind to incorporate all voices.

Chat waterfalls.

I am always thinking of different ways to invite members to participate in the mastermind. We know that everyone learns in different ways. We also know that some people are internal processors and rarely speak up unless called on or given an alternative to speaking in order to contribute.

Using an activity like a "chat waterfall" is a great way to not only invite all members to participate, but also see and hear a lot of people quickly.

In a virtual setting, a chat waterfall is easy to do. Most online meeting tools have some sort of chat function. All you do is ask a great question and tell participants to put their answers in the chat. While leaders contribute via the chat, I read what they share and add a quick idea or two explaining what I like about the comment or a question I may have about the idea.

It's also valuable to ask for a volunteer to read off responses. After everyone has typed something into the chat, the mastermind can have a discussion about what they wrote and why, or you can move on to the next agenda item.

In an in-person setting you could do this using chart paper, index cards, sticky notes, or an online survey tool where participants submit their answers while you project them. The point is to vary how you connect and communicate, incorporating all voices.

Brainwriting.

When you think of a poorly run meeting, what comes to your mind? Meetings that lack direction and an agenda? Maybe it's the meeting that accomplishes nothing, so another meeting needs to be scheduled. Or there are meetings that continue to drag on, forever, with no end in sight. Finally, some meetings are poor in quality because certain individuals dominate the discussion and suffocate the diversity of thought that exists on your team.

The idea of "brainwriting" is the solution to that last point and a strategy that we've used with great success in the mastermind.

Brainwriting is simple to do and replaces the more commonly known strategy of brainstorming.

The problem with brainstorming is threefold: the loudest voice tends to dominate, that voice (and idea) then shapes the thinking of the group, and thus the ideas of quieter members never make it to the surface for discussion.

The best organizations promote the best ideas and execute the best strategy. That can't happen if only a few people within your team or organization have the microphone.

In order to brainwrite as a group, first, share the prompt, problem, or idea you want to discuss with meeting attendees ahead of time. Ask them to develop their thoughts and write them down prior to the meeting. When everyone gathers, restate the problem, prompt, or idea to be discussed and then give equal time so that everyone attending shares their idea prior to evaluating any idea. Alternatively, you can ask everyone to turn in their ideas (without their name on their writing) and have others read or present someone else's idea to the group. The gist is that you write first and talk second in order to honor the diversity of thought in the room. We often state that the best idea should win based on merit and not on volume/frequency of talking or popularity. Brainwriting is a simple strategy for bringing this to life.

And it's a winning strategy. According to Professor Leigh Thompson, brainwriting groups generate 20 percent more ideas and 42 percent more original ideas (as cited in Greenfield, 2014).

Pass the mic.

Another strategy you can use that is similar to the chat waterfall is called "pass the mic(rophone)." This protocol is useful because it not only encourages all mastermind members to engage in a discussion topic, but it also challenges members to be fully present and actively listen.

Pass the mic means that you pick who shares next. So after one member speaks, they say, "I pass the mic to [names a new member that hasn't shared yet]." It's fascinating to see how this plays out. Do men tend to pick other men? Do people of one race pick someone of the same race?

It also encourages people (in the right environment) to be vulnerable. In a large group, it can be a challenge to remember who has shared. I tend to make a mental note, but I have also written down everyone's name on a piece of paper and placed a checkmark by their name after they've shared. The vulnerability comes in when someone who needs to pass the mic doesn't know who hasn't shared yet. This is an opportunity to ask for help, and I love it when that happens. I also force myself not to chime in and to let the group figure it out. The only time I will intervene as a facilitator is when I know someone has not shared and also has not spoken up and said "I need to go." In this situation, I "see" the member and don't let them hide before addressing whatever topic we discuss. This rarely happens, but it is something to note and prepare for.

The final tactic I want to share to build inclusive environments is the "family photo." This is a simple activity and one I considered keeping secret because it works so well.

Family photos.

Right after "new business," which is the logistics part of our meeting, we end with an activity that always leaves a smile on everyone's faces. I call it a "family photo" and learned this idea from a team of coaches I work with at the altMBA.

It's easy to do. First, we collectively decide on an idea or event that we want to act out. For example, one of our members who leads an elementary school once told a story of a kindergarten student (who was a handful) who would ask him for coffee in the morning. When

Colin told the story of this kid asking him for coffee, the mastermind was laughing so hard, half of us were in tears. So at the end of the meeting we decided we would either (a) act as if we were the kindergarten student asking the principal for coffee, or (b) act as if we were the principal in this situation. We hold the pose for five minutes and I capture a screenshot of that moment.

In the introduction I mentioned the idea of *ichi-go ichi-e*. The family photo captures the meaning of this term: "One meeting, one moment in your life that will never happen again . . . We could meet again, but you have to praise this moment because in one year, we'll have new experience, and we will be different people and will be bringing new experiences with us, because we are also changed" (Parker, 2018, p. 19).

I couldn't agree more.

Although we do the family photo at the end of every mastermind and with the same leaders of each cohort, we have changed as humans. The picture represents capturing the spirit of the moment—the moment we just shared with each other. That moment is sacred. We'll never get it back, and we'll never get a moment just like that again.

This supports an inclusive environment because every leader we support has an opportunity to set the subject for the photo. And as an actual photo, we have a record of the beautiful diverse leaders who are members in the mastermind.

In many ways, the family photo is like a mastermind yearbook that we create throughout the year.

I shared how we acted out the "coffee" scenario, but think of the wildest, weirdest, or otherwise most uncommon experience you've had in school leadership.

Now imagine reliving that experience with a group of amazing leaders, sharing a laugh, and taking a photo of that moment. That is the essence of the family photo.

If we don't act out a story from the day's mastermind, then we members just suggest something creative, such as the following:

- Act like an animal you'd see in the jungle.

- Bring a hat to the mastermind and wear it.

- What is the weirdest item on your desk?

- Pretend you are flying.

- What will your face look like on the last day of school?

You can do anything. Your only limitation is your imagination.

Note: I do not share these photos anywhere on social. They are for internal use within the mastermind. I want to keep some things special and just for our members. So I share the family photos only in mastermind newsletters and our private social channels.

If I did this in a physical setting, I would simply use a camera or smartphone with a timer on the camera, set it up to capture the group, and snap the family photo!

Intentionally building an inclusive environment supports belonging within a group. The final piece we'll look at next is the cornerstone of all healthy relationships—trust.

Nancy's Story

Nancy has been a member of the mastermind for three years. When she joined, she was an assistant principal in a large southern state. Like many of our members, Nancy grew from an assistant principal to a principal during her tenure in the mastermind. She loves the mastermind for a variety of reasons.

Recently, Nancy connected me with a high school principal and assistant superintendent within the district, both of whom became mastermind members. I love when the leaders I serve in the mastermind talk about their positive experience. The stories they share often lead to colleagues joining the mastermind as well. John, the assistant superintendent, told me that during his evaluation meeting with Nancy, she would rave about how she has grown, the support she has received, and the interesting books that she read with us. John told me that Nancy talks about the mastermind all the time when he meets with her. I realize that is probably more valuable and interesting to me than it is for you, the reader.

But here is the secret I want to share—Nancy inherited a very difficult school. It was switched from an elementary building to an all-kindergarten learning center. The teachers were upset and the culture was challenging. In fact, the majority of staff wanted to leave the school. John admitted that Nancy was given a raw deal in regard to the school she took on during her first principalship, and he confided in me that what she has accomplished in two short years is nothing less than a miracle.

Of course, Nancy is an incredibly talented and gifted leader. Many principals are, but what she had that the rest of her colleagues lacked was a personal board of directors that she met with weekly and that helped her navigate the challenges of turning a tough culture into one that is incredibly positive. Not only that, but her school is now one of the most requested schools to be transferred to! Just a couple of years ago, the staff were running out of the school to find jobs elsewhere. Now teachers run to the school because they want to be a part of something special.

Nancy had to do the work to see those kinds of results. Those results felt much more achievable with the support of a trusted group of colleagues who were all on a journey of creating similarly celebratory school cultures.

Trust

"Trust and respect people. That's how you earn their trust and respect."

— Lao Tzu

Key Ingredients to Establishing Trust

According to Brené Brown (2018), "It turns out that trust is in fact earned in the smallest of moments. It is earned not through heroic deeds, or even highly visible actions, but through paying attention, listening, and gestures of genuine care and connection" (p. 32). The mastermind works because the environment is grounded in trust and safety. This is our DNA.

As Brown points out, we don't have to overthink how we establish both.

Sometimes it is the simplest things that have the biggest impact. Brown identifies that trust is not a formula, hack, system, or grand endeavor. Trust is built in the "smallest of moments" in the mundane areas of life. If you want to build a trusting environment, give it time and be consistent. Consider your leadership presence. Would your mother be proud of how you acted in your role as a boss?

The mastermind can be boiled down to a simple formula:

> A successful mastermind = consistently showing up + truly seeing and hearing people + empathy and connection

This simple formula that we've been executing for years has helped masterminds offered at Better Leaders Better Schools thrive.

Leadership is already tough enough, and working in isolation is a recipe for failure. Add on to that the idea of leading in a context where no one truly knows who you are or what you are trying to achieve and it's no wonder that districts struggle to retain principals. In her book *Radical Candor*, Kim Scott (2019) says, "[Leaders] often feel *alone*. They feel ashamed that they're not doing a good job, sure that everyone else is doing better, and thus unable or afraid to seek help. But of course no [leader] is perfect" (p. xxix).

Consistency Is Key

Zenger and Folkman (2019) looked at data from 360 assessments of 87,000 leaders and found three elements of trust.

The first is positive relationships. Theodore Roosevelt said, "I don't care how much you know until I know how much you care." Being present in relationships and actually demonstrating that you care is the foundation of trusting relationships.

The second element of trust is good judgment and expertise. This does not mean that the leader is always right; it does mean that others place value in the leader's ideas and opinions. Leaders who are able to drive results and respond quickly to problems build trust with their teams.

The last quality is consistency.

Canadian author and coach Lance Secretan says, "Authenticity is the alignment of head, mouth, heart, and feet—thinking, saying, feeling, and doing the same thing—consistently. This builds trust, and followers love leaders they can trust."

This quote illustrates the importance of alignment between our intentions and actions. Each morning I recite my life and leadership principles so I can show up in the world that is aligned to who I am at my best. When I do this consistently, I am able to pave the way for trusting relationships.

Be Brave

In *Dare to Lead*, Brené Brown (2018, pp. 225–226) created a tool called the BRAVING inventory to facilitate team conversations around the topic of trust. According to Brown, there are seven elements to trust:

- **Boundaries:** Knowing your peers' boundaries, asking for permission, and the ability to say no.

- **Reliability:** Do what you say you'll do. Don't over-promise.

- **Accountability:** Owning mistakes and making amends.

- **Vault:** Keep information and experience shared in confidence, private.

- **Integrity:** Choosing courage over comfort. Do what is right.

- **Nonjudgment:** Asking or giving help without judgment.

- **Generosity:** Assume positive intent. Go above and beyond with your words and actions.

Brown (2018) uses this tool with her team. Members first reflect on each of the seven components of the BRAVING inventory and write responses aligned to each component. Brown uses this tool to promote discussion in a one-on-one session with her direct reports to discuss "where experiences align and where they differ. It's a relational process that, when practiced well and within a safe container, transforms relationships" (p. 225).

A number of these components are reflected in the mastermind core values and agreements. We can use a tool like the BRAVING inventory as a discussion topic within a meeting. The mastermind could explore where the members' leadership is doing well in relation to these seven components and where they might need to do some work. I'll often ask for stories and examples of success and failure in regards to this tool.

Week after week, I see our members living out these aspects of trust within the mastermind. The vault, specifically, is an important aspect within our community. Leaders bare their souls during a mastermind meeting. It's not uncommon to have information shared that is slightly uncomfortable and emotionally charged. Tears have been known to flow within the group. We've discussed before how to handle the tragic loss of life on campus.[57] A leader may struggle with the pressure of the job and may need help with substance abuse. Have you ever had to fire someone from your campus and then get a restraining order from the courts? We discuss heavy

---

[57] One leader experienced the most tragic loss I've come across. A family of seven died in a car crash. The school community lost five students in one night, and all this amidst an out-of-control pandemic.

and emotional topics within the mastermind. By agreeing that the mastermind is a safe container—a vault to process these experiences and emotions—every member agrees to keep confidential what is shared within our community.[58]

Make Friends, Turn Into Family

What percentage of your staff meetings end with, "Love you. See you next week"?

What percentage of mastermind gatherings end that way? One hundred percent.

Of course, I am proud of the results that mastermind members enjoy, but just as significant is the sense of community and connection that we have created as well.

Many organizations say that it's like a family and while that may be true for many, in the mastermind it's reality.

I didn't anticipate or design the mastermind in this way initially. It just sort of happened. What I didn't predict when I started the mastermind were the bonds that would form after meeting with the same people at the same time, week after week, for years, even in a virtual space! As Paige noted earlier in the book, many of the mastermind members have become close friends even though she has yet to meet any face-to-face.

I think this is indicative of a culture that promotes vulnerability and sharing through a safe environment.

---

[58] It's kind of like Vegas, but what we discuss in the mastermind *usually* doesn't break the law or violate a collective moral compass. Of course I'm joking, but what happens in the mastermind stays in the mastermind. This kind of support does not exist within districts, and if you feel isolated as a school leader, you certainly don't have a space like this to discuss the complexities of the role with others who sit in a similar seat.

After all, everyone is there to get better. The second-order consequence is that a tightly knit community forms when members help each other out through their challenges in a consistent format and space.

So one day, it just felt right to end the meeting with, "Love you all. Reach out if you need anything."

And that was that.

Caring communities matter. In cultures where teachers feel cared for, performance is enhanced and parent involvement is increased (van der Vyver et al., 2014, p. 63). I believe the same is true for school administrators. Because they are cared for within the mastermind, their performance is enhanced, and their community benefits.

The World Is Cold Enough

One thing about leaders with high emotional intelligence is that they are able to build positive work relationships and foster a sense of connectedness within their cultures. Carmeli and Gittell (2009) note that positive relationships at work lead to better performance in terms of both quality and efficiency (pp. 723–724).

A mistake that many leaders make is operating as a robot. By that I mean, they lead in a way that is too private, too at a distance. That limits their ability to form positive relationships at work, which then limits the effectiveness of their leadership. Van der Vyver et al. (2014) found that teacher performance declines in an environment where care is not evident (p. 62).

The mastermind is the opposite on a foundational level. A sense of belonging is a component of transformational leadership (Tafvelin et al., 2019, p. 35). Not only do we foster relationships within the community, but we also encourage our members to build strong relationships within the context of where they lead. When I reflect on the leaders who I found uninspiring, they treated me poorly and didn't communicate to me that they cared about me as an individual. They treated me as a mere worker—a cog in the system. If you find yourself saying (or thinking), "My staff needs to do (fill in the blank) because that's their job," you have work to do. Yes, educators are professionals who sign a contract to do whatever tasks are in the contract, but the contract is not enough. To motivate educators to do inspiring work, that will require warmth, connectedness, and, dare I say, love.

> To motivate educators to do inspiring work, that will require warmth, connectedness, and, dare I say, love.

Random Calls

In Chapter 3, I shared a "pulse" survey that I regularly sent the leaders I serve during the pandemic. During this challenging time, many members looked exhausted, frightened, and anxious. I knew this was an important time that required me to step up as a mentor, coach, and friend. The survey allowed me to pinpoint and prioritize who to reach out to each week.

Before using the survey, I liked to randomly call and text members of our community—this in addition to scheduled calls and coaching sessions I have with leaders. Here, it is more important to surprise and delight. There is no agenda other than to check in and let that leader know I care. Of course, if they have an issue they are working through, I am happy to listen, ask some strategic questions, and possibly offer some advice. Sometimes I also like to call and tell a terrible "dad" joke that I read recently. When people know you care, you are able to build the kind of environment where people feel safe. When leaders feel safe, they ask for the help they need, ask questions when they don't know the answer, and are willing to take risks. Trust is at the center of these calls.

Mastermind Case Study
Zetia Hogan
Principal at Foreign Language Immersion and Cultural
Studies School

"After joining the mastermind, I was involved in a supportive community of individuals who wanted deeper learning from others in the field."

Tell us what you do and what your work typically entails.

I serve as the principal of a pre-K–eighth-grade application school that focuses on the following foreign languages: Chinese, French, Japanese, and Spanish. My work typically entails daily operations; greeting scholars; breakfast/lunch duty; scheduled walkthroughs; and a series of community, leadership, instructional, and data meetings. As I complete the daily task and operational responsibilities, I model the agreements and expectations of our mission and vision.

How has the mastermind helped you?

The mastermind has helped me with my vision and focus as a school leader. I became more intentional about my professional growth and collaborative community. The mastermind exposed me to a variety of resources that assisted with efficiency, time management, and using social media as a resource.

What's the best part of the mastermind?

The community is the best part of the mastermind. Communicating and collaborating with like-minded leaders from around the country is invaluable. The mastermind community challenged me to think deeply about my approach to leadership, assisted with my creativity, and shared expertise about leadership best practices.

(Continued)

(Continued)

What is one way the mastermind has helped you approach leadership differently?

The mastermind helped me trust in my vision of leadership and be comfortable with not having all the answers. It helped me realize that it's okay not having the answers and that a good leader seeks support from the community. As a servant-leader, I began to focus on serving the school community and trusting in my approach and ability to lead a school community.

What advice would you give a leader considering joining the mastermind?

My advice is to *know* why you want to join the community. Do the office hours with Danny and ask as many questions as possible. Ultimately, you want to be open to taking ownership of your learning as a leader, and the first step is knowing why you want to become a member of the mastermind community.

Chapter 4 Reflection Questions

Do you agree or disagree that agreements are more powerful than expectations? Why?

Which of the mastermind agreements do you connect with the most? Why?

What can you commit to in order to create more inclusive environments at your school/district, at the professional development you facilitate, or even in the professional development you experience?

What does it take for you to build trust with a colleague?

Would you benefit from experiencing professional development that is more than "professional"? Are you connected to a community that has your back no matter what and will push you to be the best version of yourself? If you don't have that community, what is stopping you from finding one?

Challenge

5

> *"A podium and a prison is each a place, one high and the other low, but in either place your freedom of choice can be maintained if you wish."*
>
> —Epictetus, *Discourses* 2.6.25

Mindset

What Kind of Change Are You Committed To?

When you form a group that promises to develop the skills of leaders, you are on the hook for creating a service that produces magic. "Everyone wins when a leader gets better. Everyone wins when you get better" is the idea that guides our work at Better Leaders Better Schools. My backstory is that I was overlooked as an assistant principal. There were no avenues to grow my leadership within the larger system. This was true for principals in the district as well—only a select few were chosen to participate in a leadership program run by outside consultants. This was a systemic blind spot, and the majority of leaders at the principal level and 100 percent of the assistant principals received no district-led leadership development. What a missed opportunity!

Out of this challenge, I created my podcast in September 2015. I simply wanted to get better. That turned into leaders asking me for help and the rest is history.

I know the importance a principal plays in their building. Reid (2020) found that principal quality is fundamental to school and student success and second only to teachers in terms of positively influencing student outcomes like achievement, attendance, and graduation.

The quality of building leadership is a primary factor in the success of the faculty and students. The mastermind was created to fill the gap I felt. No leader who is hungry for development should be starving. Help is out there if a leader truly desires it.

It all starts with the leadership mindset. The beginning of this chapter will explore the importance of mindset and how we develop it via the structure of a mastermind.

Mindset Scorecard

In 2020, I wrote a new three-year vision. Part of that vision is joining a program built by Dan Sullivan at Strategic Coach. But I'm not ready to join yet; that's why it's on my vision. I need to grow in order to even be considered for their program. Dan is known for his work around the idea of a 10x life. This idea inspires me. A 10x life isn't solely focused on growing your revenue as a business. Ultimately, money doesn't buy happiness. In the context of school, neither does improving test scores, improving attendance, or reducing discipline. All of these metrics are important, but a 10x life is really about living a full life. Living with more freedom, intimacy, relationships, and so on.

To prepare for the program, I was asked to check out Dan's (2019) ebook, *The Mindset Scorecard*. He says, "Mindset is everything. It's very easy to score the external things you see . . . But what's more important is what's behind behavior" (p. 15). Another important distinction he makes regarding mindset is the importance of taking 100 percent responsibility for our thinking (Sullivan, 2019, p. 16). Why responsibility for our thinking? As Duke (2019) points out, our beliefs are what drive our actions, and this is why "learning loops" and feedback from a trusted board of advisors (like a mastermind) are essential in not only making better decisions, but also rigorously examining the assumptions and beliefs that guide the actions we make (pp. 79–81).

I set out to create a mindset scorecard in 2021 as a way to add more value to the mastermind. By reflecting on the most effective leaders in our community, I started to see some similarities. The mastermind mindset scorecard identifies twelve mindsets that the most effective leaders have. These mindsets were discussed in great detail in Chapter 2. You can see the entire mindset scorecard in Figure 5.1. Each of the twelve mindsets is scored 1–12 and has four distinct sections of quality. The higher the score, the more developed you are in that mindset. There isn't an ideal score that a new mastermind member should have. Instead, this scorecard is used as a tool. After applying to the mastermind, I reach out to a leader interested in the mastermind to schedule a conversation. Joining a powerful professional development experience like the mastermind should be a slow, deliberate process. Unlike a conference or workshop where registration is simple, joining the mastermind needs to go through stages to ensure the leader is ready to commit. There is clear value to joining the mastermind and what the community can do for a leader. During a strategy call, I want to identify how the applicant plans to serve the community as well.[59]

---

[59] Adam Grant wrote a book on this topic called *Give and Take*. A marketing expert whom I admire, Joe Polish, also wrote a book with a similar gist called *Life Gives to the Givers*. Zig Ziglar famously said, "You can have everything in life you want, if you will just help other people get what they want." That's why generosity is the first mindset on the scorecard.

Figure 5.1   Mastermind Mindset Scorecard

	1	2	3	4	5	6	7	8	9	10	11	12	NOW	NEXT
GENEROUS	You are a taker. Sharing resources is scary. You see the world in terms of scarcity.			You are a taker who sometimes gives when the outcome of generosity benefits you. You believe, "I'll scratch your back if you scratch mine."			You are a giver. Generosity comes naturally, but at a cost when you violate personal boundaries in order to help. This zaps your energy and ability to have more impact.			You see abundance everywhere. Generosity comes naturally and you look for ways to share resources. You honor individual boundaries so that you can be even more generous at appropriate times.				
HUNGER	You engage in professional development only when directed. You don't see value in opportunities that others find meaningful. You judge your peers' motives for seeking professional development.			You say "No" too easily to growth opportunities. Obstacles block you from professional development rather than opportunities to navigate around.			You invest in opportunities that require minimal resources. Social media, podcasts, & free workshops are enough for you. A lack of prioritizing your growth is hindering your ability to maximize your performance.			You search for the best growth experiences. You find creative solutions to enroll in programs you identify as worthy of investment. What fuels you is a desire to be the best version of yourself.				
WELCOMES FEEDBACK	You avoid feedback and discount the value of feedback shared with you.			You take action on feedback, but discount the value of feedback based on the messenger.			You actively seek out feedback and have developed great trust with peers who have permission to challenge you to be better.			You deliberately consider feedback and use systems to learn from both positive and negative outcomes. You have access to multiple feedback loops. You share what you are learning with your peers.				
CANDID	Your message changes based on the environment and people around. You talk out of both sides of your mouth.			You demonstrate candor with a small group of peers who are in your comfort zone.			You care personally & challenge directly but struggle to implement consistently.			You consistently care personally and challenge directly.				
OPEN-MINDED	The world is black and white. You believe you are either right or wrong. You don't interact with peers who don't share your point-of-view.			The world is black and white, but you are willing to work with others who don't share your perspective.			You see the world as more than black and white. However, you lack intentional tools to gather diverse opinions and slow your thinking down.			You demonstrate curiosity in every situation and use tools to slow your thinking and suspend judgment. You demonstrate empathy and seek out counter-narratives to balance your thinking.				
COLLABORATIVE	You work in isolation.			You collaborate when asked, but you don't actively seek collaboration.			You value collaboration and gathering people comes naturally. The groups you form are homogeneous.			You value collaboration and gathering people comes naturally. You are able to gather diverse groups of people.				
EXCELLENCE	Your work is consistently poor.			You can create excellent work with great effort. This output is inconsistent.			You do all things with excellence. This comes at a cost because you are not able to let some things go. It's hard to separate the forest from the trees.			Your goal is to do everything with excellence. You have a pre-determined list of items that must be done with excellence and are able to let go of tasks that don't matter in the "big picture."				

ANTIRACIST	You are racist.	You are willing to acknowledge that racism exists, but for you it exists in the past or in other spaces. You are unwilling to admit that racism exists where you are.	You are self-aware and see where your actions contribute to inequity. You actively seek out ways to grow and understand others from different backgrounds. You speak up inconsistently when you experience something racist.	You are self-aware and see where your actions contribute to inequity. You actively seek out ways to grow and understand others from different backgrounds. You speak up consistently when you experience something racist.	
EMOTIONAL INTELLIGENCE	When people ask who the "jerk" is in the organization, everyone says it is you.	You have either strong internal or external awareness, but you are not working at growing either of these areas.	You have either strong internal or external awareness. You actively work at strengthening your emotional intelligence.	You have both strong internal and external awareness. You actively work at strengthening your emotional intelligence. Peers come to you to learn how to grow in this area.	
OWNERSHIP	It is always someone else's fault.	You take responsibility when you are uncomfortable or forced to take responsibility because someone of authority makes you.	You take ownership when you are at fault and can do so unprompted.	You take ownership in all situations. Even when someone else is clearly at fault, you are able to iden- tify where you either contributed to the problem or where you could have done something better.	
GOALS	You lack authentic goals. If you have them at all they are done to fulfill compliance, but lack meaning for your work.	You have goals, but they are created to please others. They are what you think your boss, peers, or others you respect would want you to have.	You have clearly defined goals and work toward them. The tyranny of the urgent sidetracks your goals and you lose focus.	You have clearly defined and written goals. You share your goals and progress in public. You are able to teach others how to set and achieve goals. You demonstrate focus and urgent needs don't sidetrack what is most important.	
COMPASSION	People describe you as cold and mean.	You believe the professional and personal must be separate. There is a palpable distance between you and colleagues.	You are compassionate and bring your full self to work. However, you don't consistently share tough feedback because you care so much for others. Because of this, your motives are sometimes questioned.	You are warm and compassionate. People "know how much you care" and are open to your ideas. Because of your high regard for others you can share tough feedback. You integrate your personal and professional lives appropriately. People feel seen, heard, and connected because of your leadership.	
				COMPASSION	0
					0

The other feature that is unique to the scorecard is that it asks a leader to identify where they are performing currently and where they want to go in the future. I find that this helps frame a discussion and helps me understand how we can help a leader grow within the mastermind.

First-Year Process

Since the mastermind has been running for years, there is a good amount of cultural knowledge and inside jokes that a new mastermind member is unaware of, but would be beneficial to work on their mindset. For example, a number of books seem to be referred to often. Many school leaders are already pressed for time with the daily operations of school, and this becomes an obstacle for seeking out professional development experiences. Throw in a mastermind membership that already challenges leaders to read, and it would be insane to also include "extra" books from the past for leaders to dig into as well.

As a result, we developed a first-year process for new members to be exposed to the ideas via executive summaries, workshops, and tool kits from what we refer to as pillar content. In the first year, the pillar content would focus on four themes: creating world-class cultures (*Culture Code*), twelve practices that lead to success in life and leadership (*The Art of Possibility*), hosting transformative gatherings (*The Art of Gathering*), and designing magical moments (*The Power of Moments*).

The content from this first-year process could be considered a "master class" on its own for school leaders and is one way we overdeliver value via the mastermind experience. The knowledge and tools from this content alone will help school leaders transform their individual leadership and the communities they serve.

In addition to these workshops, new mastermind members have the opportunity to participate in two onboarding meetings that review our core values and agreements, and highlight the inner workings of the community. All of this is intentionally designed to work on the mindset of the leader and get them up to speed as quickly as possible.

Celebrate the Good Times

It's important to pause and celebrate. Many high achievers I know rarely slow down long enough to enjoy all that they've accomplished. They run from milestone to milestone without pausing to appreciate their accomplishments. Mastermind members value that we build into the structure a time to celebrate our wins. This need not be a long exercise, but should be just a few moments per member where they can reflect on their busy week and share something they're proud of in front of peers they respect. Celebration seems like a small thing, but it's not. Just like leaders who will often forego their own needs in order to take care of the people they serve, they also struggle to pause and reflect on their achievements. We do this not just to feel good; celebration actually builds resiliency as well.

All of us experience some form of imposter syndrome where we falsely believe there is something inherently wrong with us. While writing these words, there is a low-level hum in the back of my mind that whispers, "No one will care about what you're writing." For too many leaders, this is where they stop. I have learned how to overcome the imposter syndrome partly through taking the time to celebrate.[60] When I pause and note the ways I've added value through my writing, podcasts, coaching,

---

[60] When this book is ready for sale and published, I plan on celebrating by buying a 16-year-old bottle of Lagavulin, the best scotch in the world.

and so on, this gives me a list of achievements I can pull from. The gift is confidence. When I experience what Steven Pressfield calls "The Resistance" in the present, I think back to when I wrote my first book and all the people it helped. Reflecting on that milestone gives me the right and confidence to type these words. The other way to beat the imposter syndrome is to consistently show up and put in the work. Maybe what I write today won't make it into the book. That's okay. If I continue to write consistently day after day, I am bound to type some words that will inspire you to move past your own fears.

One last note on celebrations—I keep a record of what matters to leaders. When I hear about something a mastermind member cares about, I file it away. For example, Kyle is interested in the Civil War. If I send him a Civil War book or figurine at a random time, he will know how much I care. And when you can, go big! Chris finished his doctorate work and defended successfully in the summer of 2020. Chris and I have worked together for years and have spent time together in person as well. As our relationship matured, I learned that he is a Chicago Bears fan. As a native Chicagoan myself, I have to support Bears fans around the world. So when he officially became Dr. Jackson, a vintage 1984 Walter Payton Bears jersey arrived at his house with a simple note letting him know how proud of him I was. That gift meant so much to Chris.

Celebration is a mindset.

Reading Rainbows

Every book we've read in the mastermind has come from outside of education. This is an intentional choice because (a) I know that leaders are already reading much of the literature on education,[61] and (b) I want to

---

[61] Remember "hunger" in the mindset scorecard?

expose our community to the wide array of knowledge that exists *outside* of education. Why not learn from the best in other industries and figure out a way to apply that knowledge to education?

The entrepreneur, philosopher, and investor Naval Ravikant has said about reading, "The genuine love for reading itself, when cultivated, is a super-power. We live in the age of Alexandria, when every book and every piece of knowledge ever written down is a fingertip away. The means of learning are abundant— it's the desire to learn that is scarce" (Jorgenson, 2020, p. 114).

What do Oprah, Bill Gates, and Warren Buffet have in common? Yes, they're all billionaires, but they also read—a lot. Buffet reads five to six hours a day. Gates reads at least fifty books a year. Oprah credits much of her success to books (Simmons, 2020). Reading helps put a leader on a path of success. Mastermind members often comment on the books we read, citing their value and thanking me for exposing them to ideas they never would have come across.

Reading is an easy way to upgrade your mindset. Taking action on the ideas can turn you into a superstar.

So what exactly are the books that we read in the mastermind if they are solely books from outside of education? Let me highlight a handful of texts that we've read since 2016. I'll provide a short rationale of why I chose each book to illustrate the types of books we read and why we read them. I'll also include a list of *all* the books we've read since 2016 in the Resources section of the book.

Thinking, Fast and Slow By Daniel Kahneman. To be honest, this book is dense. Mastermind members either love it or hate it. But in my opinion, it is one of the most important books we've read so far in the mastermind. Kahneman explores how we make decisions and separates the brain into two systems: S1 and S2. S1 is fast, impulsive, and automatic; S2 is slow, conscious, and methodical. School leaders make countless important decisions a day; thus, it would make sense to improve the quality of decisions we make. Worth noting, Kahneman won a Nobel Prize for his work on decision making.

The Obstacle Is the Way By Ryan Holiday. Here, Holiday uses ancient Stoic wisdom and philosophy to illustrate how leaders might deal with the everyday struggles of life, especially the challenges that keep us up at night. The title is brilliant in that it distills the essence of the book. Where many leaders see an obstacle and quit, Holiday urges us to find the opportunity. The obstacle is actually the path forward. For school administrators leading in an increasingly demanding and complex role, this perspective of obstacles is helpful.

The Art of Gathering By Priya Parker. I have used examples from Parker's book throughout this text. The intentionality with which Parker approaches gatherings is nothing short of exceptional. *The Art of Gathering* helped mastermind members rethink their approach to gatherings both small and large within their school communities. If you use the methods shared by Parker, you are much more likely to create gatherings that dazzle and inspire your community.

Never Split the Difference By Chris Voss. Written by a former CIA hostage negotiator, this book is not only about negotiating, but also really about influence and leadership through deep listening. School leaders are hired to create and execute a compelling vision that cannot be accomplished without the ownership of a staff. Whether it is establishing buy-in on an idea or navigating sensitive conflicts within your school community, this book will show you how to move your ideas forward consistently.

Search Inside Yourself By Chade-Meng Tan. The author was an early employee at Google who then transitioned to designing and teaching one of Google's most popular in-house courses for its employees. The course was designed on the scientific benefits of mindfulness. The mastermind found the text accessible and an easy read. Tan explains the numerous benefits of mindfulness. School districts would profit from adding a mindfulness program for their employees because research shows it increases both job satisfaction and productivity. As an added bonus, humans who practice mindfulness have better self-awareness and handle stressful situations much more deftly as well.

Dare to Lead By Brené Brown. This is a must-have handbook for leadership. Brown masterfully puts language to the hard parts of leadership like vulnerability, courage, and trust (the same things we teach and practice in the mastermind). And speaking of language, she codifies language around the concepts in the book to help teams communicate better.

Thinking in Bets By Annie Duke. Similar in a sense to *Thinking, Fast and Slow*, this book is about decision making. Duke is a former World Series of Poker champion, and it's through this lens that she teaches the reader how to think probabilistically. This is important because as neuroscientist António R. Damásio points out, "We are not thinking machines that feel; we are feeling machines that think." In this book, Duke teaches us how to do the opposite and actually become a thinking machine, which is a useful skill in school administration.

How to Be Antiracist By Ibram X. Kendi. The murder of George Floyd in 2020 brought systemic racism, police brutality, and white supremacy to the forefront of American consciousness. Education is a cornerstone of society. We engaged in this talk to explore racism and how we could fight for equity within the schools we lead.

The Infinite Game By Simon Sinek. This text will become as popular as Sinek's *Start With Why* if it hasn't become so already. *The Infinite Game* is about the different mindsets leaders hold—either finite or infinite. This reminds me a lot of abundance versus scarcity thinking as well as making decisions for short-term benefits versus playing the long game. In short, the finite game is short-sighted and selfish. In the context of business, it leads to profit right now, but does damage to the future environment, culture, and the bottom line. In the context of school, it looks like the obsession with standardized test scores at the expense of providing a rich learning experience that produces citizens who are able to be not only productive, but agile, critical thinkers prepared for the future.

Emotional Intelligence 2.0 By Travis Bradberry and Jean Greaves. Investing in this text provides an assessment that will yield a score on the four components of emotional intelligence: self-awareness, self-management, social awareness, and relationship management. *Emotional Intelligence 2.0* is a must-read in that it not only breaks down the concepts of each component of emotional intelligence, but also provides more than ten activities to practice to grow your EQ. Why would you want to grow your EQ? The authors have tested more than half a million leaders and found that 90 percent of high performers also score high on EQ as well as make on average more than $29,000 more than their lower EQ peers in salary (Bradberry & Greaves, 2009, p. 21). In short, you'll be more effective and you could get paid better by developing your emotional intelligence. Now, I'm sure you are like me and you didn't get into education to "get rich." Money isn't what drives the average educator; it's about impact and giving back to the community. But it is possible you'll increase your salary if you improve your emotional intelligence. At the very least, you'll become more effective.

Socrates Knew a Thing or Two

The highest-quality question is an open-ended question. If you're new to leadership, you will quickly learn that many people will come to you for the answers. Sometimes you have to make the decision, providing the answer then and there. But the majority of the time, you serve your community better by answering a question with a question. I use this all the time in the mastermind to grow our leaders.

Sure, mastermind members do want to know what I think and what their peers think as well. However, it is *much* more powerful when they come to the conclusion themselves. The mastermind provides a space where they can wrestle with the challenges of leadership and get support to improve their thinking.

Whether it is answering a question with a question or beginning a discussion with a juicy open-ended question, the infinite potential embedded in asking great questions is there for any leader.

Somewhere I read a line that has stuck with me to today. The idea was simple: managers provide answers. Leaders ask great questions.

When I facilitate a mastermind, I swear that 90 percent of the time is listening, 8 percent is asking great questions, and 2 percent is reflecting what I've heard and occasionally adding my own point of view.

Here are ten "coachly" questions that I often ask:

- What is the hard part for you?

- What is the next easiest step?

- How would you coach another person facing this same challenge?

- What is the opportunity embedded in this challenge?

- Is that all? Is there anything else you'd like to tell us?

- What would you do if you weren't afraid?

- What are you most proud of in this moment?

- What do you notice?

- How could you do this in half the amount of time? How does the plan change if you take three years?

- Who is in your network that can help you?

Coaching isn't just a list of great questions to ask. It is about radical listening, reflecting back what you hear as a mirror, and personalizing each experience.

These aren't all my go-to open-ended questions, and coaching isn't just a list of great questions to ask. It is about radical listening, reflecting back what you hear as a mirror, and personalizing each experience. But one tool all great coaches and leaders have is the ability to ask open-ended questions that unlock the path forward.

Mastermind Case Study

Rosemary Bradley

Dean of School Culture, Buffalo United Charter School

Tell us what you do and what your work typically entails.

As dean of school culture, I am charged with ensuring a safe and welcoming space for students to attend every day. The best place to start is with the staff, providing resources and confidence in them so they can give their best for our children. In this virtual world, though, my role has transitioned to include supervising the distribution and management of 1:1 devices for students, and the instructional technology staff need to teach them.

How has the mastermind helped you?

I have learned from the dozen educators in my mastermind who are all doing this great work, each from a different perspective, each allowing me to learn from their experience and their mistakes. I am more confident when I have discussed my ideas with other educators and stand on solid ground as I take my next step. I can access these great people throughout the week and have grown quite fond of them over the last three years I've been in this great group.

What's the best part of the mastermind?

Two aspects vie for top billing. First is knowing that I can be vulnerable and honest about my mistakes and they will support me, and challenge me to stand up and step forward. They remind me that we will only learn from these mistakes, and help me maintain the right perspective. They care about me as a leader and a friend. Second, and equally powerful, has been the opportunity to read some wonderful books on leadership that I would never have discovered on my own, and discuss the ideas and why they matter to us as individuals and as leaders. These are powerful aspects of the mastermind.

(Continued)

What is one way the mastermind has helped you approach leadership differently?

The mastermind members are great leaders and they are all average, run-of-the-mill women and men who have made the above-average choice to seek excellence as they strive for being the best educators they can be. They have been folks just like me who choose to be ruckus makers doing great things for children. We are a tribe! I love my tribe.

What advice would you give a leader considering joining the mastermind?

If you are happy with the status quo, you need not apply. If you have all the support you need and are already being challenged to be your best, then you can skip this opportunity.

Anything else you'd like to say about the mastermind?

I look forward to connecting with my tribe every week. Hope you can join us. I look forward to meeting you.

Taking Action

"All our dreams can come true, if we have the courage to pursue them."

–Walt Disney

What Do You Invest In?

In a mastermind, your return on investment is directly proportionate to what you put in. That's why my ideal mastermind member is generous and looks for ways to add value to anything they participate in. If a leader were to join the mastermind and passively participate, if they thought they would just take notes and absorb great ideas, then their development would be predictably stunted. Action is important. Mastermind members engage by showing up to the regular meetings and participating in the discussions and activities.

Those who choose to connect with other members outside of the established hours benefit the most.

There is much room for freedom and creativity in the mastermind. Members are invited to make the spaces we occupy uniquely theirs. In some ways, mastermind engagement acts like compound interest. There is an initial investment that may feel quite demanding, but after that initial deposit, the benefits become an example of autocatalysis. The energy needed to start the reaction creates an output that then continues to feed the cycle of positive outcomes.

This may look like reading leadership texts outside of education for the first time. Then a member might take their annotations and apply what they learned more seriously. This could also look like engaging in the private channels we have for members to connect outside of meeting times or forming friendships with an individual member in a cohort before branching out.

Leaders are asked to share the facilitation responsibility of the mastermind meeting. There is a general agenda that a leader can build from, but again, leaders are encouraged to make it 100 percent their own. For the members who have stripped down the structure of the gathering and completely rebuilt it, infusing their creativity and unique perspective, those members have gotten the biggest benefit from being a leader of leaders.

Scott Constantly Takes Action

In Chapter 3, I shared Scott Long's story of taking action on the idea of "sticky core values." Scott is an incredible leader. He's one of the best I know. One thing I admire about his leadership is that he is always taking action. Not only has he transformed his elementary school's culture via sticky core values, he has started an internal mastermind for his district and used a decision-making tool I created to make a volatile staffing decision against his district's first suggestion of how to move forward.[62]

The founders of Basecamp have something to say about taking action as well. Fried and Hansson (2010) note, "We all have that one friend who says, 'I had the idea for eBay. If only I had acted on it, I'd be a billionaire!' That logic is pathetic and delusional. Having the idea for eBay has nothing to do with actually creating eBay. What you *do* is what matters, not what you think or say or plan" (p. 38).

Scott doesn't talk about the idea of eBay; he builds it. I asked him to reflect on his mastermind experience and how taking action on the ideas has improved his leadership. This is what he wrote:

When I first joined Daniel Bauer's mastermind community in November of 2018, my focus was singular and simple—to grow my own professional competencies. At that time, I was filled with self-doubt around one question: Am I really good enough and smart enough to lead my teachers, and, in turn, help our school become amazing?

I logged on to our mastermind Zooms eagerly each Wednesday night, looking for notes to take and ideas to make my own. I quickly adapted key concepts from the various

---

[62] His decision was high quality, and it led to a positive outcome as well. It impressed his central office administrative team so much, they asked where he learned how to apply logic regarding his staffing decision. "The mastermind," he said.

books we studied. I dialed in on all of the awesome tools my mastermind counterparts were using at their schools. Over time, I found myself stamping out my self-doubt.

A year later, as my competencies grew, I began to examine a different question. This question, however, challenged me to explore how I operated with the leaders within my school district, specifically my fellow elementary principals. As a collective group, we lacked collaboration, lived in a state of petty competition, and rarely challenged the status quo. And, when we did meet, we focused our time and energy on operational issues that rarely impacted culture, teaching, and learning. Our deficiencies were glaring. And yet, there I was, once again, doubting myself: Am I really good enough and respected enough to be the person that changes how we operate as a community of leaders?

One particular Wednesday night, our mastermind left me on a natural high, buzzing with excitement over a sudden realization. Somehow, it just clicked. No one person in our mastermind was the savior. No one person was the reason we all kept coming back. Rather, the magic of the mastermind was the shared sense of community and purpose. Furthermore, our framework—rotating facilitators, book studies, the hot seat, and accountability measures—ensured that we invested our time in meaningful

(Continued)

(*Continued*)

conversations and transformative learning opportunities. The smartest person in the room was, in fact, the room.

These realizations helped me confidently move forward with recommending a mastermind platform to my fellow elementary principals. In using this framework, I did not have to be the one person that changed how we operated. Instead, *we* could be the team that changed how we operated.

Thus, in September 2019, I invited my fellow elementary principals in the district on a journey to be the room. I told my mastermind story to them and explained why we should try it out. As we head into 2021, we find ourselves completing two book studies, engaging in some amazing hot seat topics, and helping each other grow. In fact, it has been the purest form of professional development accessible to us. Here's the best part. In March 2020, when COVID shut us down, our elementary principal mastermind stopped meeting. There was just too much to process. It could have easily died on the vine. And yet, when we returned to school in the fall, we all agreed on one thing: kick-starting our mastermind was a *must*.

(Long, personal communication, October 28, 2020)

Leader of Leaders

Powerful professional development is not passive; it's active. Transformation comes when leaders are asked to be a better version of themselves. Browning

(2018) identifies "Three Rules for Successfully Leading Other Leaders" in a *Forbes* article she wrote. Those three rules are: empower top talent, afford freedom through discipline, and don't forget to give challenges and feedback.

"Effective principalship involves an ongoing process of personal and professional growth and it is a professional and organizational responsibility, the hallmark of any profession, to pursue ongoing learning and development" (Bush, 2013; Hallinger & Snidvongs, 2008; OECD, 2009, all as cited in Service & Thornton, 2019, p. 3).

Following are a number of ways we promote professional growth, afford freedom through discipline, and empower our members.

Facilitate the Mastermind. Illness birthed the innovation of rotating mastermind facilitation. This exponentially increased the value of the mastermind because it challenged current members to step up and be a leader of leaders. Since I facilitated each week in the early days of the mastermind, it didn't occur to me that this was an ideal way for leaders to push their own development.

Be My Podcast Guest. I want the world to know how special mastermind members are. Sharing their stories gives practical tools for listeners of the podcasts to use in order to elevate the activity within their school communities. Making mastermind members the star of an episode is truly a feel-good experience and creates an artifact they can always point back to, share with others, and enjoy. How might you do that with your staff?

Host the Podcast. The School Leadership Series was a daily podcast I started after the Better *Leaders Better Schools* podcast in order to reach more school leaders. When challenging the mastermind to question traditions within their school, I realized I didn't have to host my own podcast. As a result, I've invited mastermind members over the years to create content that would inspire and encourage our listeners.

Contribute or Collaborate On Blogs. Our website doesn't have the same reach as the podcast, but still serves thousands of leaders each month through the content we share. This was yet another way to promote the great ideas of mastermind members and live out our motto, "Everyone wins when a leader gets better. Everyone wins when you get better."

Offer Coaching Sessions. Some mastermind members have a desire to mentor and coach other leaders. This is the ultimate way of leading leaders, so I have put together trainings, shared resources, and coordinated coaching calls so our members could give back in this way.

Co-present at Conferences and Webinars. I have co-presented a handful of times with other mastermind members at conferences and webinars in virtual and face-to-face settings.

Design New Structures. The onboarding process explained in the previous section of this chapter was designed by Paige Kinnaird. I set the vision and got out of her way. This process didn't exist without her leadership. I was the bottleneck. By casting vision and providing some feedback, I effectively removed myself from the process. As a result, a new and needed mastermind structure was born, and it was infinitely better than what I could create.

Collaborate on This Book. Mastermind members wrote their own case studies. Just like the "shared purpose" discussed in Chapter 3, this book was created with mastermind members.

Besides these intentional activities that challenge leaders to take action, there is one tool within the mastermind that we regularly use that challenges our members to level up.

The One Big Thing

The strongest form of accountability happens when it is not forced and occurs in a safe environment. We don't evaluate leaders in the mastermind—after all, everyone gets an A! When a leader knows that their peers are also their champions, the critical feedback they receive is much more palatable. This kind of feedback is regularly shared within the context of the hot seat. Another tool we use is called "The One Big Thing." The hot seat and "The One Big Thing" are also the third component of leading leaders according to Browning (2018).

This activity is simple. A leader selects what the priority is to complete for next week, writes it down, shares it in public, and asks to be held accountable for completing it. The simple act of identifying, writing down, and communicating a priority has a tremendous impact on getting it done. When I tell my mastermind peers that I want to accomplish "X," there is no chance that I'll show up the next week to tell people I lead that I didn't get "X" done. That's not going to happen.

Matthews (2015) found that people who thought about their goals were 43 percent more likely to achieve them. Those who wrote down their goals were 61 percent more likely to achieve them. People who wrote down their goals, told their friends, and shared a weekly progress report were 76 percent more likely to achieve a stated goal.

The One Big Thing is a simple tool to use to increase the productivity of the mastermind and any other group you may lead. I haven't started this yet, but I believe there is a way even to gamify The One Big Thing. Writing this last sentence, I would like to find a way to honor those who keep the longest streak alive during each quarter throughout the year.

Mindset and taking action are two challenges that help lead to transformation. The final component is the community itself.

Mastermind Case Study
Alex Fangman
Principal at Grant's Lick Elementary

Tell us what you do and what your work typically entails.

I am currently the principal of an elementary school (K–5) in rural northern Kentucky. My work primarily revolves around staff development and building school culture. In a workplace with limited resources, I serve as both an instructional coach and a principal to 25 staff members. This means that I wear a variety of other hats, but improving instructional capacity among teachers is the one that I enjoy wearing the most.

How has the mastermind helped you?

The mastermind has helped me to diversify my thought process by being able to connect with leaders from an array of backgrounds. As a result, I am able to see both problems and solutions from all sides and come to the best possible answer. Sometimes, this process occurs even when I am not the one asking a question or offering an opinion but merely listening to another person's perspective. As a result of the mastermind, I have learned to understand the many sides of running a school, and this has helped me become a greater resource to the people I serve.

What's the best part of the mastermind?

The opportunity to connect with so many talented leaders from across the globe. The principalship can be a lonely chair to sit in, especially when you're the only administrator in a building. The mastermind has allowed me to network with other administrators who act as a sounding board to challenge and broaden my thinking.

What is one way the mastermind has helped you approach leadership differently?

The mastermind has helped me realize that I am not always going to possess the perfect answer to every scenario that running a school can throw at you. Instead, it is better to help build the capacity of your people to fill in your weaknesses so that you can concentrate on your greatest strengths and leverage them to elevate your staff.

What advice would you give a leader considering joining the mastermind?

Do it! This has single-handedly been one of the most invigorating professional/personal development tools I have encountered. The fact that you have a community of leaders who not only know what it feels like to sit in your chair, but also have been in the situations you are trying to navigate, has helped give me the confidence and clarity of thought to guide my building.

Anything else you'd like to say about the mastermind?

I am thankful to be a part of a dedicated group of educators who are committed to honing their craft to impact change for their community of learners.

Powerful Community

"The toughest aspect of being a leader—hell, being an adult—is meeting the world as it is and not as we wish it to be."

—Jerry Colonna

Working Through Challenges

The greatest gift the mastermind offers is the community. Since leading in isolation is a choice, our members elect to lead in community. Sure, they have to then go into their schools and organizations and do the work, but they know each week there is a space where they can get a trusted perspective on their biggest challenges. Between meetings, members reach out to each other and collaborate as necessary.

> Since leading in isolation is a choice, our members elect to lead in community.

In the mastermind we read *The Checklist Manifesto* by Atul Gawande, who is a top surgeon in the United States. I came across an article he wrote in *The New Yorker* titled, "Personal Best." In the article, Gawande (2011) explains how ridiculous it is that doctors don't have coaches. He reflects on how we all accept that top athletes and performers have coaches, so why don't doctors? Of course, I would add, why don't principals?

If education is the foundation of society and works with each community's most precious resource—the children—schools cannot afford not to have coaches dedicated to building the capacity of building leaders. In Gawande's personal account, he shares how difficult it was to ask for help and hire a coach. He said, "Why should I expose myself to the scrutiny and fault-finding?" (Gawande, 2011).

It takes a special kind of leader to sign up to a community that will push them to be better. My assumption is that is why so many *choose* to lead in isolation. It is easier to hide, it is easier to work alone, it is easier to move fast, when it's just you. But is it effective?

"Coaching done well may be the most effective intervention designed for human performance. Yet the allegiance of coaches is to the people they work with; their success depends on it. And the existence of a coach requires an acknowledgment that even expert practitioners have significant room for improvement" (Gawande, 2011).

Blue Pill or Red Pill?

Duke (2019) also identifies the importance of surrounding yourself with others if you want to make better decisions. "To get a more objective view of the world, we need an environment that exposes us to alternate hypotheses and different perspectives" (p. 138). The only way to upgrade our thinking is by joining a powerful community.

"We don't win . . . by being in love with our own ideas" (Duke, 2019, p. 130). If leaders truly want to transform, they need to seek out a network of people who are willing to challenge their decisions and leadership. Annie Duke calls this kind of community a "truth pod" and likens its value to the story of *The Matrix* to drive her point home. In that movie, Neo is offered a blue pill or a red pill by Morpheus.

"You take the blue pill, the story ends. You wake up in your bed and believe whatever you want to believe. You take the red pill, you stay in Wonderland and I show you how deep the rabbit hole goes," says Morpheus (Wachowski & Wachowski, 1999). If you have seen *The*

Matrix, you know that Neo chooses the red pill and his eyes are opened to the world as it really is, not how he wishes to see it. This is the point of the mastermind.

School leaders lack access to outside perspectives and community. This lack of access also impacts the quality of leadership in schools. The constant busyness of day-to-day operations doesn't allow for critical dialogue that will challenge leaders to grow (Forde et al., 2013, p. 108). Collaboration is essential to leadership reform, and programs offered within a district often harm leadership performance by supporting the status quo (Sherman, 2005, pp. 709–710).

Duke (2019) identifies three aspects that make a truth pod (or mastermind) effective:

- A focus on accuracy (over confirmation)

- Accountability

- Openness to a diversity of ideas (p. 130)

Pure Gold

These three components are essential to an effective mastermind and are the cornerstone to its most effective tactic, the "hot seat," which we'll look at in detail next.

There is great value in a mastermind membership—the powerful network one joins immediately, the consistent mentoring and growth, and the resources shared generously between members. But the greatest value is in what I call the hot seat.

When I describe mastermind membership and the hot seat, I usually say, "Imagine having a personal board of directors on speed dial that can help you solve any problem." That is what it's like to participate in a mastermind and engage in the hot seat. The hot seat is so valuable, it is the only thing that doesn't change from mastermind meeting to meeting. I give free rein to and encourage facilitators to reimagine how we gather, but the one thing that must be protected is the hot seat time.

The hot seat is often the most transformational experience in the mastermind. Forde et al. (2013, p. 108) found that coaching offers the gift of space and time for interconnection, reflection, unconditional listening, and the opportunity to focus on one's own needs. The frantic pace of school leadership rarely allows leaders to pause, breathe, and reflect on their performance, their challenges, or their vision. We know that school leadership is incredibly isolating as well. The mastermind and hot seat force this issue. Because of the cohort model built on mutual respect, trust, and safety, the hot seat leads to professional breakthroughs frequently. Leaders invest good money into this experience, and the hot seat is one of the most valuable times. Where else can a school leader get focused, uninterrupted, challenging feedback shared from a place of mutual respect and candor? Where else do school administrators go to admit what they don't know without fear of repercussion?

There is incredible value in sitting on the hot seat and absorbing the knowledge, experience, stories, and questions of your mastermind peers. Interestingly, members' time off the hot seat can actually be *more* valuable for two reasons:

- It feels great to help someone else through generosity and sharing of your experience.

- It is helpful to be either reminded of past challenges that you need to be ready for or prepared for new challenges you didn't even know existed.

By hearing the hot seat questions of your peers, you walk away from every mastermind meeting with a more holistic approach to your leadership. You have more tools for your tool belt, and your leadership development is accelerated because you absorb the collective knowledge and experience of all of your mastermind colleagues.

It would take an individual leader years to learn what a mastermind member can gain after a few months of high-level discussion and engaged participation.

In the next two sections, I will share how we run the hot seat, but the gist is this—an individual leader explains their problem and leverages the collective IQ and experience of their colleagues to solve the problem. In addition to challenges, a member might describe a project or goal they are hoping to achieve. In this situation, the mastermind will help them get started and help them build momentum before starting.

Hot Seat Protocol 1

Ninety percent of the time we run the hot seat in the following way. The leader on the hot seat shares the context of their problem or describes a project they want to launch in the near future. Ideally they take as little time as possible (three to five minutes) to describe their challenge, giving just enough context that their peers can understand their situation. Some leaders take too long to describe their problem and speak for far longer than five minutes. This is a problem because it limits the feedback and ideas they can get from their peers. It helps to remind the leader sharing to keep it short, providing just enough context for the group. If a member is still long-winded, then gently interrupt and nudge them on so the mastermind can provide value.

> It would take an individual leader years to learn what a mastermind member can gain after a few months of high-level discussion and engaged participation.

After the leader shares their predicament or project, the rest of the mastermind speaks up. All eyes are on the hot seat leader and all comments directed to them. The mastermind is now getting hot! Leaders might ask clarifying questions during this time, share wonderings, tell anecdotes of success, or share what they've learned if they have been in a similar situation and failed.

As the facilitator, I love to see how the group is generous during this time, offering sage advice and building on top of one another's ideas. If time allows, it is smart to ask the leader on the hot seat what they found most valuable and how they plan to take action.

Pitfall #1: Sometimes the hot seat leader feels a need to justify or begins to take things personally. Again, if they talk too much, they aren't getting peer coaching. There is value in self-reflection for the hot seat member, and I believe it is valuable for mastermind peers to hear how leaders process their challenges, but if this dialogue shifts to justification, move things along as the facilitator.

Pitfall #2: Watch out for dominant figures in the mastermind. Some members talk more than others. It's the facilitator's responsibility to make sure everyone is providing feedback and value. A facilitator can call on quieter members or invite them to put comments in the chat in a virtual setting (or write a note in a physical setting).

Pitfall #3: Time. It's easy to run out of time on the hot seat. Sometimes hot seats have a nice break point within the fifteen- to twenty-minute window. A leader on the hot seat may even stop the group and say, "Thanks. This has been really helpful. I have what I need and we can move on." But most of the time the mastermind is in rhythm. Like a great concert, you don't want the hot seat to end, but it needs to. What helps me in these situations is believing that although more can be shared, what was discussed during the allotted time was enough.

Hot Seat Protocol 2

My friend, Kyle Wagner, introduced a great protocol for the hot seat.[63] The mastermind loved this second protocol because it challenges the leader on the hot seat to remain silent while the rest of the master-mind discusses the challenge as if that leader is not there. Here is how to run this second protocol for the hot seat.

Step 1: Prepare the tuning session.

- Organize the discussion so everyone can see each other.

- Ensure a presenter and facilitator have been appointed.

- Share (or screen share) relevant materials associated with the dilemma.

- Establish/remind all participants of the norms.

Step 2: Introduce the dilemma.

- The presenter introduces and provides an overview of the dilemma (background of problem, associated con-text, supporting artifacts).

Step 3: Ask clarifying questions.

- Group asks clarifying questions of the presenter so that they may have a clearer understanding of the challenge presented by the leader on the hot seat.

---

[63] This process was inspired by the National School Reform Faculty protocols available at nsrfharmony.org.

Step 4: Ask probing questions.

- Group asks probing questions of the presenter. These are used to help the presenter deepen their thinking about their particular dilemma.

Step 5: Discuss.

- The presenter takes notes during the discussion.

- The facilitator begins the discussion with supportive feedback and then transitions to opportunities for solutions/growth.

Step 6: Respond.

- The presenter has the opportunity to respond by sharing what struck them and what new perspectives they have.

Step 7: Debrief.

- The facilitator leads a conversation debriefing the process.

(Wagner, personal communication, June 25, 2019)

Think About It

Despite my best efforts to overcommunicate, some members show up to the hot seat unprepared and waste a fantastic opportunity to level up. Most members are keenly aware of what their biggest challenges are and can improvise a question that will serve them well. My experience has taught me that members who take ten to fifteen minutes to dig deep into their current challenge are better prepared for their time on the hot seat and extract their maximum value.

What follows are some questions I send to members the week of their hot seat in order to help them prepare.

Questions to consider for the hot seat

1. What professional challenge is keeping me up at night?

2. What is a personal goal or challenge that's keeping me up at night?

3. What project/initiative/idea would I love to get off the ground, but I could use help with the next step or I would benefit from a brainstorm session?

4. What gives me anxiety when I think about it (could be a task, event, or individual)?

5. What is one area/skill/trait I'd like to develop more?

6. What is a topic I'm interested in and the mastermind could help accelerate my understanding of?

7. What questions or topics do I find fascinating and would love to hear what mastermind members also think?

8. What am I currently procrastinating on?

9. What have I been hiding that I just haven't asked for help with yet?

The hot seat leverages the power of a community of leaders coming together with the shared purpose of getting better. This is the most valuable aspect of what we do in a mastermind next to plugging in to a diverse network of other school leaders from around the world. The hot seat and other discussions happen within the context of a mastermind meeting. Those conversations then go offline and the learning continues. By working on the mindset, encouraging our members to take action, and providing a powerful community to support a member's leadership development, the last component of the ABCs is formed.

Mastermind Case Study

Nick Hoover
Founding Principal at Cantwell's Bridge Middle School

"Darkness cannot drive out darkness, only light can do that. Hate cannot drive out hate, only love can do that."

–Dr. Martin Luther King, Jr.

Tell us what you do and what your work typically entails.

I am the principal of a middle school in Delaware. I am leading our building through change with a firm hold on our core values. I also lead several district-level workgroups and committees. As a leader, I am constantly learning, reflecting, leading, and reflecting again.

How has the mastermind helped you?

The mastermind has provided me with a network of other leaders to collaborate with, share with, reflect with, and learn with. Most importantly for me, I am always looking to be challenged. I don't want a group of people to just shake their heads and agree with everything I say. I want to be challenged on my thinking and actions so I can, in turn, reflect and grow.

What's the best part of the mastermind?

I love sharing ideas, situations, and advice in my mastermind. I get the opportunity to hear others' stories and challenges and help provide some ways that might improve the situation. But I also get the chance to share my struggles or ideas and get their feedback.

What is one way the mastermind has helped you approach leadership differently?

My group has a diverse approach to thinking. They come at situations from different angles, often ones I don't think about. This allows me to step back and reflect as I go into a situation where I need to lead other people with diverse perspectives.

(Continued)

(*Continued*)

What advice would you give a leader considering joining the mastermind?

Do it! Get on board and then open your mind.

Anything else you'd like to say about the mastermind?

I will never go without a mastermind again.

Chapter 5 Reflection Questions

Where do you currently score on each component of the mindset scorecard? Where do you want to score next? How will you get there?

What was the last book you read *outside* of education that made you better?

Do you read enough? If not, what's stopping you?

Do you struggle with celebrating? One way to build motivation and purpose toward achieving a goal is to preplan and visualize how you will celebrate once you achieve your desired goal. What would it look like to add a celebration to a goal you are currently pursuing?

What is an idea (like eBay, but in the context of school) that you have been putting off? What is an idea that would benefit from you taking action?

What holds you back from taking action on big ideas? How can you move past those upper-limit challenges?

Do you have a powerful community to plug in to? One that is rich in experience and diverse in worldview? If not, where can you plug in to a community like that? What is the cost of not finding that community?

Conclusion

///

"Infinite minded leaders understand that 'best' is not a permanent state. Instead, they strive to be 'better.' 'Better' suggests a journey of constant improvement and makes us feel like we are being invited to contribute our talents and energies to make progress in the journey" (Sinek, 2019, pp. 56–57).

The Only Game Worth Playing

The quote from Simon Sinek's *The Infinite Game* sums up perfectly the game all school leaders are playing, whether they know it or not. It is absolutely the game we are playing in the mastermind. It is tempting to brand the mastermind as the "best" professional development available for school leaders, but the truth is, it's not. The mastermind is a great opportunity for the right school leader. The ideal member described in Chapter 2 and the mindset scorecard described in Chapters 2 and 5 are two helpful indicators of whether the mastermind would be a good opportunity for you. If you connected with the ideas in this book, then an experience like the mastermind would be right for you as well.

What I can say with 100 percent accuracy is that the mastermind is a *powerful* professional development experience because it is built on the ABCs: authenticity, belonging, and challenge. When I reflect on the professional development I experienced over the years, the ABCs were either lacking entirely or only somewhat visible. Keeping our focus on authenticity, belonging, and challenge inspires life and leadership transformation. Although we aren't perfect, the mastermind is really, *really* good. Every day we strive to be better, and we invite our members to help make that dream a reality. Our members are authors of their own leadership journey; we're glad we get to participate in the adventure.

A Brief Look Back

This book focused on the mastermind as a professional development opportunity and on what makes it a unique experience for many school leaders across the globe.

In Chapter 1, we looked at the variety of reasons school leaders aren't experiencing transformative professional development. Some professional development is delivered inauthentically. Isolation is a key reason that leaders don't connect and grow. Many districts do their best, but the professional development they offer ends up being missed opportunities.

Chapter 2 previewed the mastermind experience, including an ideal member and the ABCs of powerful professional development™: authenticity, belonging, and challenge. In my view, professional development built with the ABCs in mind leads to transformation.

Chapter 3 was a deep dive into authenticity. Professional development that is psychologically safe, encourages self-awareness, and is values-driven can be regarded as authentic.

Chapter 4 focused on belonging. Shared purpose, inclusive environments, and trust are the cornerstones of creating connection between leaders in a professional development experience.

Chapter 5 addressed how the mastermind challenges its members to level up. We do this by developing our leaders' mindsets, encouraging them to take action, and surrounding them with a powerful community.

An Invitation

This book argued that the biggest problem facing school leadership is the lack of access to high-quality professional development. When leaders lack access to high-quality professional development, they become less confident. And when leaders are less confident, they make poor decisions. Finally, when leaders make poor decisions, their individual effectiveness decreases, but ultimately the community and students suffer.

That's the bad news.

The good news is that there is a better way, and it's in your power to change. You can *choose* a different path.

The mastermind is built on the ABCs of powerful professional development™, and you can choose to join an established mastermind community or take the ideas in this book and start your own.

Leaders who join a mastermind live out our motto: "Everyone wins when a leader gets better. Everyone wins when you get better." When a leader is more successful, they take more risks, they're willing to stretch, and they don't fear failure because they know failure is a great teacher. And when a leader takes more risks, stretches past their comfort zone, and learns from failure, then they are not only learning and growing, but also able to create the ideal future of education that they dream about.

If you'd like to experience the ideas in this book for yourself and test the transformative power of our community, then I invite you to apply to the mastermind we offer at Better Leaders Better Schools. You

can do so by visiting https://betterleadersbetterschools
.com/mastermind-application or sending an email to
mastermind@betterleadersbetterschools.com. We will
open as many cohorts as needed to live out the BLBS
Just Cause "to connect, grow, and mentor every school
leader who wants to level up."

Keep making a ruckus!

Mastermind Case Study

Jason Dropik
Head of School at Indian Community School

"Adversity does not build character, it reveals it!"
—James Lane Allen

Tell us what you do and what your work typically entails.

I serve as the Head of School for the Indian Community School, which
is a private four-year-old kindergarten through eighth-grade school
that serves students of American Indian descent. I am in charge of
programming, budgeting, school operations, cultural integration, and
community communication.

How has the mastermind helped you?

The mastermind has been foundational for my leadership growth. It
has helped me to get objective opinions and ideas from educational
thought leaders throughout the country. It has helped me in having more
than ten instructional and leadership coaches by creating a network of
individuals I can support and lean on to continue to grow. They are
not connected to my school community so they can provide unbiased
feedback and ideas that have helped me grow as a leader and person.

The mastermind has also provided opportunities to engage in
professional reading that supports continued expansion of thoughts

and ideas on education, life, and leadership. Engaging in book studies that are relevant and purposeful helps me be a better person and leader. I get to hear about others' successes and challenges so that I know I am not alone. The mastermind has increased my confidence as a leader so that I can take on the diverse challenges and support the needs of my community.

What's the best part of the mastermind?

The best part of the mastermind is the community we have that is supportive, creative, and compassionate. The mastermind members can relate to the challenges that exist and provide perspectives and encouragement to face the challenges that present themselves to educational leaders. I am thankful for the insights and passion that we collectively experience.

What is one way the mastermind has helped you approach leadership differently?

The mastermind has helped me by challenging me to approach leadership in innovative ways that challenge the status quo. The mastermind has enabled me to see that there are many options in every situation. Leadership is not linear, so there is no one way to get to a positive outcome for students or staff.

What advice would you give a leader considering joining the mastermind?

If a leader is considering joining the mastermind, I would advise them to see that investing in their growth will help them improve as a leader. Joining the mastermind will help them to have a team of coaches, mentors, and friends who want nothing more than to see them succeed. If a leader is hesitant because they are not sure what they will get or what they can provide, they should lean in to that uncertainty because they will see immediately how everyone benefits from the group. We are all stronger together than we are individually.

(Continued)

(Continued)

Anything else you'd like to say about the mastermind?

The mastermind's benefits were beyond what I ever imagined. The group motivates me to be a better leader. I am able to share successes and receive support in overcoming adversity. In the educational landscape, the more perspectives and experiences that we are able to expose ourselves to, the better equipped and prepared we are to thrive no matter what is in front of us. I would not be where I am today without the mastermind. It has been the greatest decision I have made in my educational journey, and the benefits continue to fill me with such a strong feeling of gratitude and hope.

Resources

//

Ruckus Maker, here you will find additional resources I mentioned throughout the book. If you prefer a digital copy for download, you can get those free on my website at https://betterleadersbetterschools.com/master-mindbook. You also might find a few more bonuses, including some writing that didn't make it in the final draft of this book.

A Simple Opening Activities Checklist

☐ Does this activity invite leaders to express themselves authentically?

☐ Does this activity foster more belonging within our community?

☐ What challenge is embedded in this activity?

☐ What emotions do I want leaders to experience after engaging in this activity?

☐ What change do I hope to inspire by using this activity?

☐ Have I run this activity before? What did I learn the last time I facilitated? What does "better" look like this time around?

☐ Can leaders easily take this activity and share it with their faculty?

Every Book We've Read in the Mastermind Since 2016

"Today a reader, tomorrow a leader."

–Margaret Fuller

The mastermind is much more than a book club, and the books we read are selected to expose members to the wealth of wisdom found outside of education. In this list, you'll find every book we've read in the mastermind since 2016. Only two books are specific to education. The list can be used as course material in any leadership development class. You can't go wrong with any book on this list, and the books do not appear in a specific order. Use this list as a checklist. I also challenge you to apply what you learn and to create even more impact by teaching what you've learned to someone else.

Essentialism by Greg McKeown

Creativity, Inc. by Ed Catmull and Amy Wallace

Switch by Chip and Dan Heath

Procrastinate on Purpose by Rory Vaden

Good Leaders Ask Great Questions by John Maxwell

What Great Principals Do Differently by Todd Whitaker

The 12-Week Year by Brian Moran

Miracle Morning by Hal Elrod

The Go-Giver Leader by Bob Burg and John David Mann

Deep Work by Cal Newport

Ego Is the Enemy by Ryan Holiday

Leadership Step by Step by Joshua Spodek

Never Split the Difference by Chris Voss and Tahl Raz

The Happiness Advantage by Shawn Achor

Thinking, Fast and Slow by Daniel Kahneman

The Power of Moments by Chip and Dan Heath

The Art of Possibility by Rosamund Stone Zander and Ben Zander

Great at Work by Morten Hansen

The Better Leaders Better Schools Roadmap by Daniel Bauer

When by Daniel Pink

The Culture Code by Daniel Coyle

Emotional Intelligence 2.0. by Travis Bradberry and Jean Greaves

Measure What Matters by John Doerr

Dare to Lead by Brené Brown

The Big Leap by Gay Hendricks

The Infinite Game by Simon Sinek

Radical Candor by Kimberly Scott

Thinking in Bets by Annie Duke

Thanks for the Feedback by Douglas Stone and Sheila Heen

Stillness Is the Key by Ryan Holiday

BIPOC-Authored Books

Search Inside Yourself by Chade-Meng Tan

The Checklist Manifesto by Atul Gawande

The Art of Gathering by Priya Parker

How to Be an Antiracist by Ibram X. Kendi

Caste by Isabel Wilkerson

The Person You Mean to Be by Dolly Chugh

Decision Journal

Part 1: Prepare

Decision number:

Date:

Time:

Decision:

Mental/physical state:

☐ Energized	☐ Focused	☐ Relaxed
☐ Confident	☐ Tired	☐ Accepting
☐ Accommodating	☐ Anxious	☐ Resigned
☐ Frustrated	☐ Angry	☐ Other

Part 2: Set the Context

The situation/context of my challenge:

The variables that may influence the outcome:

What additional complexities do I see?

What are people I trust saying about this decision?

Part 3: Explore Options and Decide

Describe all of your options:

What I expect to happen and the actual probabilities of each option:

(If you could use some coaching on how to "think in bets" and use probabilistic thinking, this blog post and free download is for you: https://www.betterleaders-betterschools.com/second-order-thinking/)

The option I chose:

What does this analysis *not* tell us?

Part 4: Review

Review date (6 months after the decision date):

What happened and what I learned:

(Adapted from Parrish, 2014)

Reference List

Adams, M. (2009). *Change your questions, change your life: 10 powerful tools for life and work* (2nd ed.). Berrett-Koehler.

American Psychological Association Zero Tolerance Task Force. (2008). Are zero tolerance policies effective in schools? An evidentiary review and recommendations. *American Psychologist, 63*(9), 852–862. doi:10.1037/0003-066X.63.9.852

Aurelius, M. (2003). *Meditations* (G. Hays, Trans.). Modern Library. (Original work published ca. 161–180)

Authentic leadership: What it is, why it matters. (2020, November 17). Center for Creative Leadership. https://www.ccl.org/articles/leading-effectively-articles/authenticity-1-idea-3-facts-5-tips/

Ball, D. (2021, January 27). *An evening at dinner scenario.* [Mastermind presentation].

Bauer, D. (2020, March 19). Mastermind agreements. *Better Leaders Better Schools.* https://www.betterleadersbetterschools.com/mastermind-agreements/

Bauer, S. C., Silver, L., & Schwartzer, J. (2019). The impact of isolation on new principals' persistence: Evidence from a southern US state. *Educational Management Administration & Leadership, 47*(3), 383–399. doi:10.1177/1741143217739359

Bonchek, M. (2013, March 14). Purpose is good. Shared purpose is better. *Harvard Business Review.* https://hbr.org/2013/03/purpose-is-good-shared-purpose? registration=success

Bond, B., Quintero, E., Casey, L., & Di Carlo, M. (2015). *The state of teacher diversity in American education.* Albert Shanker

Institute. https://www.shankerinstitute.org/resource/teach erdiversity

Bradberry, T., & Greaves, J. (2009). *Emotional intelligence 2.0*. TalentSmart®.

Brown, B. (2018). *Dare to lead: Brave work. Tough conversations. Whole hearts.* Vermilion.

Browning, S. (2018, July 27). Three rules for successfully leading other leaders. *Forbes.* https://www.forbes.com/sites/forbeshu manresourcescouncil/2018/07/27/three-rules-for-success fully-leading-other-leaders/

Carmeli, A., & Gittell, J. H. (2009). High-quality relationships, psychological safety, and learning from failures in work organizations. *Journal of Organizational Behavior, 30*(6), 709–729. doi:10.1002/job.565

Chandler, S. (2015). *Crazy good: A book of choices.* Maurice Bassett.

Clear, J. (2018). *Atomic habits: An easy and proven way to build good habits and break bad ones.* Random House Business Books.

DeHaas, D., Akutagawa, L., & Spriggs, S. (2019, February 5). *Missing pieces report: The 2018 board diversity census of women and minorities on Fortune 500 boards.* Harvard Law School Forum on Corporate Governance. https://corpgov.law .harvard.edu/2019/02/05/missing-pieces-report-the-2018-board-diversity-census-of-women-and-minorities-on-for tune-500-boards/

Delizonna, L. (2017, August 24). High-performing teams need psychological safety. Here's how to create it. *Harvard Business Review.* https://hbr.org/2017/08/ high-performing-teams-need-psychological-safety-heres-how-to-create-it

Doerr, J. (2018). *Measure what matters: How Google, Bono, and the Gates Foundation rock the world with OKRs.* Portfolio/Penguin.

Duke, A. (2019). *Thinking in bets: Making smart decisions when you don't have all the facts.* Portfolio/Penguin.

Eblin, S. (2017, October 12). *Coaching your clients to lead and live at their best.* [Full summit notes]. Seventh Annual World Business Executive Coaching Summit.

Edmondson, A. (1999). Psychological safety and learning behavior in work teams. *Administrative Science Quarterly, 44*(2), 350–383. doi:10.2307/2666999

Epictetus. (2014). *Discourses, fragments, handbook.* (R. Hard, Trans.). Oxford University Press. (Original work published ca. 108)

Forde, C., McMahon, M., Gronn, P., & Martin, M. (2013). Being a leadership development coach: A multi-faceted role. *Educational Management Administration & Leadership, 41*(1), 105–119. doi:10.1177/1741143212462699

Fuller, E. & Young, M. D. (2009). *Tenure and retention of newly hired principals in* Texas. Texas High School Project. https://www.casciac.org/pdfs/ucea_tenure_and_retention_report_10_8_09.pdf

Frankl, V. E. (2006). *Man's search for meaning: An introduction to logotherapy.* Beacon Press. (Original work published in 1946)

Fried, J., & Hansson, D. (2010). *Rework: Change the way you work forever.* Vermilion.

Gallwey, T. (2015). *The inner game of tennis: The ultimate guide to the mental side of peak performance.* Pan Books. (Original work published 1975)

Gawande, A. (2011, October 3). Personal best. *The New Yorker.* https://www.newyorker.com/magazine/2011/10/03/personal-best

Greenfield, R. (2014, July 29). Brainstorming doesn't work; try this technique instead. *Fast Company.* https://www.fastcompany.com/3033567/brainstorming-doesnt-work-try-this-technique-instead

Hansen, M., & Quintero, D. (2018, November 26). *School leadership: An untapped opportunity to draw young people of color into teaching.* Brown Center Chalkboard. https://www.brookings.edu/blog/brown-center-chalk

board/2018/11/26/school-leadership-an-untapped-oppor tunity-to-draw-young-people-of-color-into-teaching/

Hiatt, B. (2018, February 20). Laverton school principal Trish Antulov found dead at her desk. *The West Australian*. https://thewest.com.au/news/education/laverton-school-principal-trish-antulov-found-dead-at-her-desk-ng-b88 751137z

Hill, N. (2005). *Think and grow rich*. Jeremy P. Tarcher/ Penguin. (Original work published 1937)

Holiday, R. (2016). *Ego is the enemy*. Portfolio/Penguin.

Jain-Link, P., Kennedy, J. T., & Bourgeois, T. (2020, January 13). 5 strategies for creating an inclusive workplace. *Harvard Business Review*. https://hbr.org/2020/01/5-strategies-for-creating-an-inclusive-workplace

Jorgenson, E. (2020). *The almanack of Naval Ravikant: A guide to wealth and happiness*. Magrathea.

Kahneman, D. (2011). *Thinking, fast and slow* [eBook edition]. Farrar, Straus, and Giroux.

Kahneman, D., & Tversky, A. (1979). Prospect theory: An analysis of decision under risk. *Econometrica, 47*(2), 263. doi:10.2307/1914185

Levin, S., Leung, M., Edgerton, A. K., & Scott, C. (2020, October 21). *Elementary school principals' professional learning: Current status and future needs*. Learning Policy Institute & NAESP. https://learningpolicyinstitute.org/sites/default/files/product-files/NAESP_Elementary_ Principals_Professional_Learning_REPORT.pdf

Matthews, G. (2015). *Harvard goals research summary*. https://www.dominican.edu/sites/default/files/2020-02/ gailmatthews-harvard-goals-researchsummary.pdf

Ng, S., & Szeto, S. E. (2016). Preparing school leaders: The professional development needs of newly appointed principals. *Educational Management Administration & Leadership, 44*(4), 540–557. doi:10.1177/1741143214564766

O'Neill, M. R., & Glasson, S. (2018). Revitalising professional learning for experienced principals: Energy versus ennui.

Educational Management Administration & Leadership, 47(6), 887–908. https://doi.org/10.1177/1741143218764175

Parker, P. (2018). *The art of gathering: Create transformative meetings, events, and experiences.* Portfolio Penguin.

Parrish, S. (2012, April). *This is water by David Foster Wallace* [Full transcript and audio]. Farnam Street. https://fs.blog/2012/04/david-foster-wallace-this-is-water/

Parrish, S. (2014, February). *Creating a decision journal: Template and example included.* Farnam Street. https://fs.blog/2014/02/decision-journal/

Parrish, S., & Beaubien, R. (2018). *The great mental models: General thinking concepts* (Vol. 1). Farnam Street Media Inc.

Parrish, S., & Beaubien, R. (2019). *The great mental models: Physics, chemistry and biology* (Vol. 2). Latticework Publishing.

Reid, D. B. (2020). US principals' sensemaking of the future roles and responsibilities of school principals. *Educational Management Administration & Leadership, 49*(2), 251–267. doi:10.1177/1741143219896072

Rozovsky, J. (2015, November 15). *The five keys to a successful Google team.* Re: Work. https://rework.withgoogle.com/blog/five-keys-to-a-successful-google-team/

Scott, K. (2019). *Radical candor: Be a kick-ass boss without losing your humanity* (rev. ed.). St. Martin's Press.

Seneca. (2004). *Letters from a Stoic.* (R. Campbell, Trans.). Penguin. (Original work published ca. 63–65)

Service, B., & Thornton, K. (2019). Learning for principals: New Zealand secondary principals describe their reality. *Educational Management Administration & Leadership, 49*(1), 76–92. doi:10.1177/1741143219884673

Sherman, W. H. (2005). Preserving the status quo or renegotiating leadership: Women's experiences with a district-based aspiring leaders program. *Educational Administration Quarterly, 41*(5), 707–740. doi:10.1177/0013161x05279548

Simmons, M. (2020, February 25). Bill Gates, Warren Buffett, and Oprah all use the 5-hour rule. Here's how this powerful habit works. *Business Insider.* https://www.businessinsider.com/bill-gates-warren-buffet-and-oprah-all-use-the-5-hour-rule-2017-7

Sinek, S. (2019). *The infinite game.* Portfolio/Penguin.

Sullivan, D. (2019). *The mindset scorecard.* The Strategic Coach Inc. https://resources.strategiccoach.com/quarterly-books/the-mindset-scorecard

Superville, D. (2017, March 8). Few women run the nation's school districts. Why? *EducationWeek®.* https://www.edweek.org/leadership/few-women-run-the-nations-school-districts-why/2016/11

Tafvelin, S., Hasson, H., Holmström, S., & Schwarz, U. V. (2019). Are formal leaders the only ones benefitting from leadership training? A shared leadership perspective. *Journal of Leadership & Organizational Studies, 26*(1), 32–43. doi:10.1177/1548051818774552

van der Vyver, C. P., van der Westhuizen, P. C., & Meyer, L. W. (2014). Caring school leadership: A South African study. *Educational Management Administration & Leadership, 42*(1), 61–74. doi:10.1177/1741143213499257

Wachowski, L., & Wachowski, L. (Directors). (1999). *The matrix* [Film]. Warner Bros.

Women in management: Quick take. (2020, August 11). Catalyst. https://www.catalyst.org/research/women-in-management

Young, G. F., Scardovi, L., Cavagna, A., Giardina, I., & Leonard, N. E. (2013). Starling flock networks manage uncertainty in consensus at low cost. *PLoS Computational Biology, 9*(1). doi:10.1371/journal.pcbi.1002894

Zander, R., & Zander, B. (2002). *The art of possibility* (reprint ed.). Penguin.

Zenger, J., & Folkman, J. (2019, February 5). The 3 elements of trust. *Harvard Business Review.* https://hbr.org/2019/02/the-3-elements-of-trust

Index